THE LURE OF LITERACY

THE LURE OF LITERACY

A Critical Reception of the Compulsory Composition Debate

MICHAEL HARKER

STATE UNIVERSITY OF NEW YORK PRESS

Published by
State University of New York Press, Albany

Printed in the United States of America

For information, contact
State University of New York Press, Albany, NY
www.sunypress.edu

Production, Laurie D. Searl
Marketing, Kate R. Seburyamo

Library of Congress Cataloging-in-Publication Data

Harker, Michael, 1976–
The lure of literacy : a critical reception of the compulsory composition debate / Michael Harker.
pages cm
Includes bibliographical references and index.
ISBN 978-1-4384-5495-5 (hardcover : alk. paper)
ISBN 978-1-4384-5494-8 (pbk. : alk. paper)
ISBN 978-1-4384-5496-2 (ebook)
1. English language—Composition and exercises—Study and teaching. 2. English language—Rhetoric—Study and teaching (Higher) 3. Literacy. I. Title.
PE1404.H3625 2015
808'.042071—dc23 2014009553

10 9 8 7 6 5 4 3 2 1

CONTENTS

ACKNOWLEDGMENTS

A Georgia State University PAWS Junior Teaching Release allowed me the time and resources to finalize my book for publication. Work on this project was also supported by a Georgia State University Research Initiation Grant, a Georgia State University Department of English Summer Research Award, and a Hambidge Artist in Residence Fellowship. Previous versions of certain portions of my book appeared in the journal *Literacy in Composition Studies* (LICS). I am grateful to LICS for granting me permission to reprint material from my study, "The Legibility of Literacy in Composition's Great Debate: Revisiting 'Romantics on Writing' and the History of Composition."

In the process of writing this book I have spoken about my ideas, questions, and struggles with mentors, colleagues, and friends. I offer my special thanks to Beth Burmester, Shawn Casey, Daniel Coe, Kathryn Comer, Scott Lloyd DeWitt, Aman Garcha, Susan Hanson, Mary Hocks, Ashley Holmes, Nan Johnson, Stephen Johnson, Andrew Kopec, Aaron McKain, Debra Moore, Rupesh Naik, Mary Ann Norfleet, Caitlin Ryan, Craig Teel, Tom, Vicki, and Aminda Warburton, and Gerry Weber.

I am grateful to Randy Malamud, my department chair, who read and commented thoughtfully on several chapters of this book and guided me through the proposal process and several grant and award applications. Thanks also to colleagues who reviewed my manuscript and provided suggestions, especially Kelly Bradbury, Lindsay Dicurci, Lyneé Lewis Gaillet, Baotong Gu, Tim Jensen, George Pullman, Susan Kates, Cindy Selfe, H. Louis Ulman, and Wendy Wolters-Hinshaw. Special thanks go to Mike Bierschenk and Laurie Searl for their close readings of every chapter and editing of the manuscript.

Beth Bouloukos, my editor at SUNY Press, advocated for this project from the beginning, and with the help of Rafael Chaiken guided me through the publication process. I am very appreciative of the support I have received from SUNY Press, especially from the two anonymous reviewers of my manuscript, who provided detailed, constructive, and encouraging feedback.

As readers will see, I owe a great debt to Harvey J. Graff who introduced me to the field of literacy studies and took an interest in my work, encouraging me to think more broadly, comparatively, and historically about composition studies and the field's investment in myths and legacies of literacy. I am also grateful to Kay Halasek, who introduced me to the Great Debate over compulsory composition and provided thoughtful direction of my program of study while I was a graduate student at The Ohio State University. I am especially appreciative of Harvey and Kay for their willingness to co-chair my dissertation, out of which this book grows. Although my understanding of literacy has evolved since graduate school, I also wish to acknowledge the University of Oklahoma's Composition, Rhetoric, and Literacy program. Michael C. Flanigan, David Mair, Catherine Hobbs, Susan Kates, Ron Schleifer, Kathleen Welch, Karen Jobe, and Ron Brooks were among the very first to ask me to define literacy and attempt to understand how characterizations of literacy impact the teaching of composition.

I also wish to express my gratitude to Dr. Seth Walker and his fine staff at the Emory University Adult Cystic Fibrosis Clinic in Atlanta, Georgia. Since receiving my diagnosis and learning how to manage complications that come from living with CF, I have developed a new appreciation for many things in my life. To be sure, I cherish each day that I breathe freely, especially those days when I find myself surrounded by friends and family. But I am especially appreciative of physicians like Dr. Walker who are working to improve the day-to-day lives of people with CF in its varying forms.

Finally, I am deeply grateful to my parents, Ralph and Linda Harker, and my sister, Elizabeth Hylton, for their encouragement and support during the writing of this project. I dedicate this book to them.

INTRODUCTION

A NECESSARY BEGINNING

> In the face of confusing challenges and at a time of disconcerting societal and global transformations efforts evoking "functionalities" and "non-functionalities," "cultural" and "historical literacy," canons old and new, skills of survival and of humanity speak to the same conclusions: the legacies of literacy must be reconsidered and literacy/literacies reconstructed. That would provide a necessary beginning.
>
> —Harvey J. Graff, *Literacy and Historical Development: A Reader*

Complaints about compulsory first-year writing are numerous and familiar: If acceptable habits of reading and writing have not been attained before students enroll in college, composition will prove ineffective for these students because one or two semesters of composition instruction are not enough to improve students' writing, reading, speaking, and thinking. Graduate teaching assistants are characterized as lacking both the experience and the intellectual and professional preparation to do the job. Students enrolled in the course supposedly lack motivation because the subject is compulsory, or they feel as though they are simply repeating high school assignments. The compulsory nature of the course strains English departments' personnel resources, thereby undermining the morale of teachers whose time would be better spent teaching something else.[1] Taken together, these criticisms aimed at compulsory composition form what Leonard Greenbaum calls "The Tradition of Complaint," a series of assaults against freshman English that began in the late 1880s and continues in various forms today.

Given that complaints about compulsory composition and proposals to abolish it seem to "ebb and flow," as Robert Connors suggests, in response to world wars, perceived literacy crises, and other legislative, economic, and academic pressures; it is understandable that questions and confusion remain about the relationships between this debate and significant moments in the history of higher education. After all, the theoretical underpinnings and rationales for compulsory composition in higher education take shape alongside and in relationship to the complaints and pressures that seek to reform, change, and (in many cases) abolish it altogether. Whether these pressures grow out of the emergence of land grant and co-education colleges during the 1860s, the transformation of colleges from the classical curricular model to the elective system during the late nineteenth century, or the drastic changes that World War II brought to general education courses in the mid-1940s, freshman composition continues to reflect the aspirations of the universities that teach it. If this is the case, complaints about compulsory composition and proposals for its abolition are also linked to the history of the American college in profound ways.

The Lure of Literacy disentangles persistent complaints about the aims and effectiveness of composition from the history of higher education. In doing so, it underscores how the relationship of freshman composition to literacy, language acquisition, formal schooling, and higher education is a fundamentally complex one. Contemporary receptions of this debate have oversimplified these relationships. Although no foundational text on the debate over compulsory composition exists, Robert Connors's article, "The New Abolitionism" comes closest. In it he suggests that complaints about freshman composition are symptoms of more general social, ideological, and cultural trends. In addition, Connors's account records the complex and sustained history of the debate, but questions remain, especially with respect to underlying attitudes about literacy: How do scholars advocating abolition of compulsory composition characterize literacy? To what extent do definitions of literacy vary across proposals to abolish and reform freshman English? In what ways do arguments on all sides of the debate depend on notions of literacy crisis and decline? How might this debate function as a site for exploring the actual and ostensible differences that grow out of the institutional contexts of literacy among students, teachers, and administrators?

David R. Russell's characterization of literacy and its role in the debate over composition's abolition raise similar questions. "Romantics on Writing: Liberal Culture and the Abolition of Composition Courses" is less comprehensive than Connors's examination; it focuses on two proposals for the abolition of compulsory composition: Thomas L. Lounsbury's in 1911 and Oscar James Campbell's in 1939. In his often cited essay, Russell analyzes the arguments that the two abolitionists "used to attack" freshman composition and explores some of their underlying assumptions. For Russell, these assumptions are tied to what James A. Berlin describes as "Brahminical romanticism," a culture opposed to the "democratic, vocational, and scientific orientation" of universities during the period of academic specialization between 1870 and 1920 (Russell 133). It is important, according to Russell, to explore liberal culture as an underlying assumption of opposition to freshman composition because these assumptions continue "to fuel the conflicts within English studies" between what he understands to be "teachers of literature and of literacy" (132). To be fair, it should not come as a surprise that concerns about literacy remain implicit orientations for Russell's and Connors's studies. Neither author sets out to address this aspect of the "Great Debate" specifically. Connors aspires to situate complaints about compulsory composition in historical, social, and economic contexts. Russell delineates the fundamental characteristics and origins of liberal culture, connecting consequences of this movement to attacks against compulsory composition. Thus, when literacy is addressed in these studies it is done so in anecdotal and figurative terms.

For example, in speculating about connections between reformist periods and attitudes about literacy, Connors notes that during reformist periods, freshman composition is seen as the "thin red line protecting the very life of literacy" (3). Connors's propositions are compelling, but the implications of such statements remain unclear because literacy itself remains uncomplicated in Connors's inquiry.[2] Connors and Russell do not associate varied attitudes about the uses, abuses, and functions of literacy with proposals for composition's abolition. As such, the appeal—or lure—of compulsory composition instruction is exclusively linked to literary and educational movements like Romanticism, the rise of liberal culture, and the politics of English studies, rather than the overriding influence of both English instructors' and students' abiding belief in literacy acquisition to realize the aims of higher education more generally. Furthermore, existing accounts of the "Great Debate"[3] do not explore how different conceptualizations of literacy, specifically those understandings that exaggerate the powers of literacy, have informed attempts to reform and change freshman composition on both theoretical and practical levels. Also absent from examinations of the abolition debate are explorations of the overlapping cultural, intellectual, and social pressures from the history of higher education in the United States.

More recently, however, David Fleming's *From Form to Meaning: Freshman Composition and the Long Sixties, 1957–1974* establishes promising links between attitudes about literacy and the history of freshman composition, especially complaints about the course's effectiveness. *From Form to Meaning* is primarily concerned with the events surrounding the remedialization of English 101 and subsequent abolition of English 102 at the University of Wisconsin–Madison in 1968. In his introduction, Fleming discusses how the general public's anxiety "about the ability of young people to write correctly and well" (4) has regularly manifested itself in the form of literacy crises.

Fleming rightly connects these crises to a host of cultural and economic pressures, arguing that "anxiety about adolescent writing" is persistent (even "perpetual") and that "changes in the economy, society, and culture do appear to exacerbate that anxiety" (8). In the end, however, even though Fleming speaks to the ways that literacy crises provoke educational reforms (4) and unnecessarily burden young writers (8–9), his interest in literacy seems restricted to noting that literacy crises are ever-present. I do not dispute this fact, and I believe Fleming's study to be an invaluable resource for understanding the circumstances behind the events that occurred at the University of Wisconsin in the late 1960s. That said, I believe a prolonged examination of latent attitudes and definitions of literacy in specific proposals for composition's abolition and reform can offer teacher-researchers even more, especially in terms of understanding why the debate over composition has persisted for so long.

Speaking to issues at the heart of scholarship in composition studies, the history of higher education, and literacy studies, this book argues for a different understanding of the "Great Debate" than existing studies. By locating, naming, and connecting latent definitions and attitudes about literacy that inform proposals for composition's abolition to theories of language and an expanded historical context, this project explains how and why literacy itself has come to, in Stephen North's words, "loom" over freshman composition (375). I argue that is by enlarging the historical context of this debate—a distinctive characteristic of the New Literacy Studies' methodology—that we understand why proposals to abolish compulsory composition have foundered. After all, as Michael Moghtader reported in a 2001 national survey of the first-year composition requirement, despite predictions of its demise and countless calls for its abolition, the requirement of freshman composition is "a stronger presence today" than it was in the past, certainly stronger than Ron Smith predicted it would be in his national survey completed in 1974. Smith concluded his study by asserting that his findings "point to more schools dropping the composition requirement, more diminishing of the one that exists," but he could not have been more wrong. Fleming agrees, writing, "The fact is, despite the dramatic changes in literacy that have taken place over the last century, the course's anomalous situation internationally, and its awkward fit even in the U.S. academy, first-year writing continues to be very widely taught in the United States and, increasingly, beyond" (3). Examining attempts to understand literacy—its meaning, powers, and the consequences of possessing it—in the context of the debate over compulsory composition sheds some light on why.

In sum, *The Lure of Literacy* challenges teacher-researchers who presume that the topic of literacy is "well-traveled" ground in rhetoric and composition scholarship. If this is the case, I argue that it is perhaps the most compelling reason for renewed interest in literacy studies, specifically the ways in which the literacy myth intersects with the day-to-day work of teaching composition. My investigation demonstrates that significant assumptions about literacy inform all perspectives that constitute the debate over compulsory composition. In most cases, these assumptions are based on frail and ambiguous conceptualizations of the nature of literacy. These conceptions often emphasize the "strong, uniform, universal, unitary, unwavering nature and impact" of literacy (Graff, *Literacy and Historical Development* 19). As my study will demonstrate, regardless of the position scholars take in the debate—as reformists or abolitionists—they share much in common when it comes to confiding in conceptions, or as Harvey J. Graff terms them, the "continuities and contradictions" of literacy. Consequently, though many have participated in and examined the great debate over composition—while this ground is in fact well-traveled—because we have not acknowledged the role of myths and "legacies of literacy" in the debate, as a field, we know little about why the ground we have traveled looks the way that it does.[4] In making assumptions, definitions, and attitudes about literacy more legible in proposals to both reform and abolish compulsory composition, a great deal is at stake. We may find a way out of an unproductive and cyclical debate that returns us time and time again to the same starting point: criticizing composition instructors and students for not achieving the impossible and pursuing the ostensible problem(s) of illiteracy with mismatched solutions.

With these stakes in mind and in the chapters that follow, I reframe the Great Debate over compulsory composition with an eye toward literacy. Chapter 1 demonstrates how exaggerated expectations of the powers of literacy underline calls to abolish compulsory composition. Employing New Literacy Studies' precepts, I reread some of the first printed calls to abolish compulsory composition. I show how the period of academic specialization (1865–1920) and exaggerated understandings of the ostensible powers of literacy inform these proposals, complicating attempts to bring about lasting reform in the teaching of composition. Chapter 2 supplements existing histories of the abolition debate by incorporating overlooked voices of both abolitionism and reform. I question the validity of a distinction posited by contemporary receptions of the abolition debate, namely, between "abolitionists" and "reformists." My view is that this division is only possible if we ignore persistent continuities in the debate, especially with respect to the tendency to situate literacy as independent and neutral variable in processes associated with human cognition. In chapter 3, I challenge dominant narratives of abolitionism in composition by examining proposals that seek not to abolish the requirement but to reform the course on various levels. Taken together, these essays demonstrate that, like abolitionists, arguments employing the rhetoric of "cooperation," "continuity," and "reform," rely on problematic attitudes about literacy as well. Chapter 4, focusing primarily on Sharon Crowley's well-known proposal to abolish the universal requirement of composition, is situated more specifically in the context of materialist critiques of the conditions of teaching writing. By examining the rhetoric of academic discourse surrounding Crowley's call to abolish compulsory freshman composition, I explain how her proposal has gained currency in English studies. This chapter argues that her role in the abolition debate deserves greater critical attention, if only for the explicit attention she gives to literacy in her seminal study. My final chapter takes up Stanley Fish's *New York Times* op-ed piece, "What Should Colleges Teach?" (2009) and his book-length examination of higher education, *Save the World on Your Own Time*. I contend that Fish's polemics on composition rehearse the same arguments and criticisms that have been levied against composition since its inception. What is revealed by my examination of Fish's critiques is that although literacy is one of the principal ends of composition theory and application, attitudes about literacy's powers, purposes, and position in academia and society at large remain unacknowledged and misunderstood, especially in our current moment.

As recently as June 2013, The American Academy of Arts and Sciences (AAAS) released a report entitled, "The Heart of the Matter." In it they call for a recommitment to a "broad, comprehensive, and balanced" educational approach, one that they describe as "distinctly American." The authors point to several reasons for renewed interest in the liberal arts and the humanities more generally. Chief among these is "Parents are not reading to their children, as frequently as they once did." According to the commission asked to compile the report on behalf of the AAAS, this statistic, coupled with declining training for K-12 teachers and reduced funding for international training programs, holds "grave, long-term consequences for the nation" (Report).

As my examination of the Great Debate will reveal, perennial notions of crisis and decline go hand-in-hand with imprecise definitions of literacy, exaggerated claims about the powers of literacy, as well as the tendency to confide in literacy myths. Such tendencies underlie the logic of proposed solutions in the AAAS's report as well. The commission's most prominent solution to problems facing the humanities is to "Support full literacy as the foundation for all learning." Despite the commission's intention to rearticulate the relevance of the humanities, the report actually invokes an ambiguously defined and empty call for "full literacy," a proposition that, in the end, seems mismatched to the problems at hand. The NLS, specifically Harvey J. Graff's work on the literacy myth, teaches us that empty calls for educational reform often function as red herrings for matters that are more deserving of our concern. The AAAS's call for "full literacy" is ostensibly effective because it resonates with the general public's desire for easy answers to educational challenges; however, it does little to attenuate or explain the disturbing consequences of shrinking state budgets, which strike more directly and effectively at the heart of the matter.

Grandiose educational reforms linked to vaguely defined terms and exaggerated expectations about literacy should remind us of why examining the history of composition from the perspective of the New Literacy Studies is so important. The debate over compulsory composition—indeed, the history of composition itself—can function as a sort of laboratory to examine, test, and explore how definitions of literacy emerge from, overlap with, and contest institutional, cultural, and economic contexts. Rereading the debate over compulsory composition from the perspective of the New Literacy Studies not only opens up new lines of thinking about the authors' historical contexts, but it also reminds us to sharpen our understanding, attitudes, and most importantly, the definitions of literacy that we rely on to face the challenges of composition instruction today. With these challenges in mind, I turn, in the conclusion of this book to a series of learning outcomes and lessons that may be used to inform a new model for first-year writing, one based on interrogating the very idea of literacy itself.

ONE

THE LURE OF LITERACY

> Literacy is not the only problem, nor is it the only solution.
>
> —Harvey J. Graff, *The Labyrinths of Literacy*

> We want to believe that every American needs to know how to read and write. The result is that no academic topic seems quite so durable a legislative—and media and popular—concern as America's apparently chronic literacy crisis: the real or imagined breakdowns in the reading and writing that we consider so central to the successful operation of our democracy. With that sort of presence always looming over Composition, anything can happen.
>
> —Stephen North, *The Making of Knowledge in Composition*

In *Writing from These Roots*, John Duffy defines literacy as a "constituent of rhetoric, a communicative modality, a technical contrivance for disseminating the version of reality preferred by a given institution, culture, group, or individual" (200). Throughout his study he posits a "rhetorical approach" to literacy, noting that such a perspective considers the "ways with words" used "in literacy instruction, especially the imposed and inherited words that shape the ways in which students and teachers think, talk, and write" (201). On the one hand, Duffy sees literacy as a part of rhetoric—the means through which one becomes more persuasive or achieves particular ends. In this sense, literacy may be understood as a discrete act, intended to move a particular audience to a specific type of action. On the other hand, Duffy's latter statement speaks to a view of literacy that sees it as an end in and of itself. In this broader context, literacy is sometimes characterized as a perspective with complex connections to cultural and political systems and ideologies. I foreground my study in Duffy's definition of literacy because his characterization of it reveals the complexity of understanding the fundamental nature of literacy as well as the consequences of possessing and providing access to literacy.

Freshman English is caught in a similar position when it comes to defining its aims and understanding its history. In various ways and at various times, compulsory composition is understood as embodying the aspirations of universities more generally. At other times, it is seen as a specific gate-keeping mechanism, an instrument (among many) through which educational aims are achieved. Similarly, the proposals to abolish freshman English that I examine in this chapter treat freshman composition as both the means and the end of higher education. Unlike current understandings of these proposals, which characterize these abolitionists as elitist and committed to the guiding tenets of liberal culture, I argue that contradictory definitions and attitudes about literacy and the consequences of possessing it are these proposals' predominant traits. In neglecting the role of these definitions and assumptions about literacy in the abolition debate, proposals to abolish composition have been evaluated in terms of their ability to realize their stated aims. This is significant: proposals to abolish compulsory composition have failed time and time again, and even though the studies discussed in this chapter are examined in both Connors's and Russell's histories of the abolition debate, they have been largely ignored in English studies more generally. As I argue throughout this book, we may repair a broken and critical connection to composition's past by demonstrating how characterizations and attitudes about literacy stand prominently among other expectations and concerns related to the history of higher education.

In this chapter, I re-read two proposals for the abolition of compulsory freshman English: Thomas Lounsbury's "Compulsory Composition in Colleges" in 1911 and Oscar James Campbell's "The Failure of Freshman English" in 1939. In "Romantics on Writing," David Russell examines both Lounsbury and Campbell; he argues that Romanticism and liberal culture are the driving forces behind these studies. I take up the same studies in this chapter because I wish to show how the New Literacy Studies (NLS) provides a generative theoretical lens through which to consider the Great Debate. By locating, naming, and connecting latent definitions and attitudes about literacy that inform these proposals to theories of language, we better understand why literacy remains composition's most pressing problem *and* solution. Toward this end, I begin by reviewing principal contributors and tenets of the New Literacy Studies. Particular discussions in this field emphasize perspectives and definitions of literacy that function as productive lenses through which to interpret proposals to abolish freshman English. That said, the following discussion is not meant to be a concluding statement on literacy or the NLS in this project. In fact, each chapter of *The Lure of Literacy* attends to attitudes, uses, myths, definitions, and characterizations of literacy.

LITERACY STUDIES AND THE ABOLITION DEBATE

One of the reasons literacy presents so many challenges to English studies is because, despite prevailing wisdom, it does not *belong* to English studies nor to any of its subfields. Literacy is similar to other critical terms like "narrative," "interpretation," or "ethics" in the sense that it is simultaneously at home and without a home, always traversing the many fields and disciplines that attempt to pin it down, define it, and give it meaning. However, what makes literacy different from these expressions is that more often than not, teacher-researchers characterize, employ, and understand literacy in terms of the perceived consequences of possessing it. Nowhere are the implications of this move for composition studies more clearly delineated than in Stephen North's *The Making of Knowledge in Composition: Portrait of an Emerging Field.*

North argues that the field of composition is comprised of distinct communities with incongruent philosophical, evidentiary, and methodological commitments. This methodological diversity reveals a lack of continuity in research and teaching practices, contributing to an overall feeling of "centerless-ness" in the field. Although many scholars criticize North for the artificiality of the methodological communities he constructs, as well as questioning many of his conclusions, North uncovers assumptions about literacy that should influence research and teaching in composition. For instance, in the conclusion to his study, North laments the consequences of assumptions about literacy, noting, "We want to believe that every American needs to know how to read and write. The result is that no academic topic seems quite so durable a legislative—and media and popular—concern as America's apparently chronic literacy crisis: the real or imagined breakdowns in the reading and writing that we consider so central to the successful operation of our democracy. With that sort of presence always looming over Composition, anything can happen" (375). I believe North refers to the field's commitment to literacy in this way—in terms of "presence"—because he wishes to highlight the nebulous and vague pressures this learning outcome exerts on composition. North suggests that although literacy, broadly defined, is one of the principal ends of composition theory and application, attitudes about literacy's powers, purposes, and position in the field remain unacknowledged and misunderstood. To understand more clearly how assumptions about literacy may magnify the sensations of "centerless-ness" that North describes in his study, we must first identify and examine some of the prevailing assumptions that surround literacy and its presumed powers, particularly since these assumptions are implicit and unacknowledged orientations for many calls for reform and change in composition, especially those calls connected to abolitionism. One of the most problematic assumptions about literacy is informed by speculation about the ostensible consequences of possessing it. In such cases, I argue that literacy itself is misunderstood, and amidst this confusion literacy gains extraordinary power as a symbol.

Little doubt exists that debates over the differences and similarities between oral and literate cultures have, in part, helped to shape scholars' attitudes about literacy in English studies more generally. At the center of this debate is Goody and Watt's "The Consequences of Literacy." In this often cited study, the authors argue that the invention of the Greek alphabet led to specific consequences: most notably, transformations on the cognitive level that are symptomatic of a shift from mythical to logical thought. The authors also claim that this cognitive shift produced a host of other social developments, including, the rise of democratic systems of government; the development of various forms of social and political organizations; and the capacity for technological progress. For Goody and Watt, cognitive capacities in oral societies are best described as lacking objectivity and relying on formulaic and associative systems of meaning making. When describing how oral societies transmit a "cultural repertoire," they write: "In the first place, it makes for a directness of relationship between symbol and referent. There can be no reference to 'dictionary definitions,' nor can words accumulate the successive layers of historically validated meanings which they acquire in a literate culture" (29). In other words, because oral cultures depend entirely on "vocal inflections and physical gestures" to communicate, they are unable to obtain distance from words and their referents.

In this claim, we find the assumption (one of many) that supports the dichotomy that Goody and Watt construct between oral and literate cultures. Oral societies lack the cognitive capacity to gain the type of critical distance that allows for a conceptualization of the world that is represented as separate from the moment. Simply put, oral cultures are forever tied to the present. In arguing for the "general differences" between oral and literate cultures, the authors assert, "writing establishes a different kind of relationship between the word and its referent, a relationship that is more general and more abstract, and less closely connected with the particularities of person, place and time, than obtains in oral communication" (44). With this presumption, the perceived ability to represent cognition as something removed from the present—as being able to achieve more objective, critical, and analytical perspectives—becomes one of the defining qualities that distinguishes literate societies from oral ones.

One of the most instructive examples of how this debate from literacy studies informs composition comes from Mike Rose's "Narrowing the Mind and Page: Remedial Writers and Cognitive Reductionism." In this study, Rose attends specifically to the problems posed by "great divide" characterizations of literacy, as well as some of its myths and legacies. Rose's chief concerns are the "troubling consequences" (287) that stem from applying "strong" versions of literacy (like those relying on a "great divide" or "grand dichotomies") to the theory and practice of basic writing instruction. In so doing, "adolescents and adults are thought to bear cognitive resemblance to (ethnocentric notions of) primitive tribesmen in remote third-world cultures" (287). The tendency, Rose argues, is for composition instructors who subscribe to "great divide" theories to draw generalizations from exceptional cases. These generalizations lead to disturbing conclusions: basic writers lack the cognitive ability to think analytically; they lack critical distance from their own lives and are thus tied socially and philosophically to the present; they believe printed words are concrete things; they are not capable of thinking abstractly about the world they live in (287). Interestingly, and as I will demonstrate, these conclusions are similar to the critiques of freshman composition that have served as the rationales for many calls for the abolition of the first-year requirement.

In addition to attending to the orality/literacy debate, Rose's essay also delineates a recurring undercurrent that traverses both literacy studies and composition. When "strong theories" of literacy form the theoretical framework for writing pedagogy, such approaches are often symptomatic of a teaching disposition that is asking too much of literacy. In *National Literacy Campaigns and Movements: Historical and Comparative Perspectives*, Robert F. Arnove and Harvey J. Graff write: "To ask of literacy that it overcome gender discrimination, integrate a society, eliminate inequalities, and contribute to political and social stability is certainly too much" (27). In a similar fashion, Rose is cautious in his treatment of literacy, noting that he does not "mean to deny the profound effects literacy can have on society" (287). Rather, he aspires to question the extent to which "great divide" theories of literacy can evaluate and describe those effects. As Rose suggests, the most pressing danger for writing instructors teaching with simplistic conceptualizations of literacy and its consequences is the tendency to assume that merely possessing textbooks, classrooms, technology, and a "trained" instructor is, as Graff writes, "fully sufficient for further development of an individual's literacy and subsequent education, and, of course, for the advancement of that individual" (27).

Many scholars in the New Literacy Studies take issue with "great divide" characterizations on both theoretical and methodological levels. For example, Sylvia Scribner and Michael Cole's exploration of the social practices of the Vai people of Liberia, detailed in "Unpackaging Literacy," questions many of the epistemological assumptions that define "great divide" positions. The authors argue that, rather than assume universal consequences of literacy, one must investigate the specific social contexts in which literacy is used. As such, Scribner and Cole's methodological approach is significantly different from Goody and Watt's. By combining anthropological field-work with psychological research methods, the authors conclude that "literacy-without-schooling is associated with improved performance on certain cognitive tasks" (136) and that many of the cognitive consequences posited by Goody and Watt are symptomatic of the formal institution of schooling rather than the acquisition of literacy alone. In short, Scribner and Cole question characterizations of literacy that position it as a monolithic symptom of social and psychological change. In so doing, they confront accumulated assumptions about literacy—Harvey Graff calls these the "legacies" of literacy—that inform many of the tenets that support "great divide" characterizations of literacy.

The implications of Graff's work for the compulsory composition debate are most clear in his discussion of the literacy myth. In *The Labyrinths of Literacy*, Graff writes that "Constituting much of what I call literacy's central contradictions, these legacies taken together constitute 'the literacy myth'" (324). Relying on the accumulation of many assumptions about the aims and uses of literacy and inextricably linked with perennial complaints of the "decline" and "crisis" of literacy, the "literacy myth" is a powerful and complex force. Defined broadly, the literacy myth is the abiding belief that merely acquiring literacy guarantees economic prosperity as well as "access to and participation in mainstream institutions" (Cushman et al. 12). In *The Literacy Myth: Cultural Integration and Social Structure in the Nineteenth Century*, Graff defines it more specifically: "Primary schooling and literacy are necessary, it is so often repeated, for economic and social development, establishment and maintenance of democratic institutions, individual advancement, and so on. All this, regardless of its veracity, has come to constitute a 'literacy myth'" (xxxviii). Using a comparative and sociohistorical research methodology (examining, among other things, Canadian census data from the nineteenth century), Graff demonstrates that despite institutionally sponsored efforts to legitimize the myths and legacies of literacy, societies have taken different "paths" toward achieving literacy. Furthermore, they have done so for reasons other than improving their economic and material situations.

Despite the growth of literacy studies in recent years, some scholars question many of the theoretical and methodological underpinnings of this movement. Most notably, in "A Critical Discussion of the 'New Literacy Studies,'" Kate Stephens reexamines the claims of central figures in this movement. In Stephens's understanding the New Literacy Studies, as "exemplified in the work of Street, Heath, Gee, Barton and others, takes a sociocultural view of literacy, emphasizing the description of literacy practices of everyday life, and challenging approaches which emphasize decontextualised basic skills" (10). Upon reviewing and critiquing the central tenets of this movement, Stephens concludes her article by proposing an approach to literacy that is, in her words, "normative," and that "allows the particular cognitive importance of literacy, and a valuation of the teacher's role in skill development" (11).

Of particular interest to Stephens are Brian Street's efforts to deconstruct the claims for literacy that constitute what he describes as the "autonomous" model. In "What's 'new' in New Literacy Studies?" (2003), Street explains that his work "begins with the notion of multiple literacies, which makes a distinction between 'autonomous' and 'ideological' models of literacy" and "develops a distinction between literacy events and literacy practices" (77). According to Street, prevailing characterizations and attitudes are based on the assumption that "literacy in itself"—i.e., autonomously—"will have effects on other social and cognitive practices" (77). This model hides cultural and ideological assumptions, and as a result imposes Western attitudes about literacy on other cultures and groups in such a manner that makes literacy acquisition and its consequences appear neutral. "Research in the NLS," Street reports, "challenges this view and suggests that in practice literacy varies from one context to another and from one culture to another and so, therefore, do the effects of the different literacies in different conditions" (77). This perspective, on the other hand, is consistent with the "ideological" model of literacy. For Street, this model represents a more "culturally sensitive" approach that views literacy as rooted in social practices and varying across contexts. As such, attitudes and understandings of literacy from the ideological perspective begin with questions about its nature and the values that shape these understandings. That is, as Street reports, literacy "is not simply a technical or neutral skill," (77) and it is "always contested" (38).

Stephens's and others' criticisms of the NLS, however, oversimplify the complexity and variability of literacy as it relates to issues of attainment as well as more general expectations that shape both theories of learning and public policy. And though Stephens does not say so directly, her objections to ideas that "underpin the 'New Literacy Studies'" (10) leave the impression that she would take issue with the underpinnings of critical literacy as well. Of the thematic commitments related to the New Literacy Studies, critical literacy has enjoyed perhaps the most thorough consideration by teacher-researchers in English studies (this is one reason why critical literacy is not discussed at length in this book).[1] Nevertheless, Ira Shor's "Our Apartheid: Writing Instruction and Inequality" is particularly relevant to my argument because of the way in which Shor brings critical literacy perspectives to bear on questions related to writing instruction.

More than other examinations of compulsory composition, Shor's study succinctly reveals the complex relationship between material conditions surrounding instruction and basic writing specifically. And although Shor acknowledges critical literacy's roots in the work of Antonio Gramsci, Paulo Freire, and others, he also emphasizes that concerns about power relations, language, and education are endemic to the work of composition studies itself (92). He reminds readers that Sharon Crowley, Jim Berlin, Donald Stewart, Bob Connors, Mina Shaughnessy, and Susan Miller have all labored to complicate prevailing and dismissive attitudes about writing instruction. He remarks on how, from composition's inception, unequal power relations have led to a subordination of writing to reading (92). Refuting the claim made by some that compulsory composition possessed a democratizing function, he instead characterizes composition as a "part of the undemocratic tracking system pervading American mass education" (93). Furthermore, he questions specifically the dubious relationship between skills-based conceptions of learning in basic writing courses and maintaining "an unequal status quo" (94). And, in the end, Shor urges us to stop turning a blind eye to the "immoral conditions" surrounding compulsory basic writing—to do away with the "mechanism that functions to ease the growing conflict between corporate and economic policy and a mass of aspiring students who are being deterred from the democracy and from the American Dream" (95).

One implication of Shor's characterization of basic writing is that he suggests that regressive attitudes about literacy (in particular skills-based conceptions) are symptoms of undemocratic practices, unfair working conditions, and the more general immoral conditions surrounding the compulsory composition machine. Proponents of critical literacy have provided ample evidence that this is in fact the case. However, Shor's discussion of basic writing is, in a sense, addressing a larger matter. Regressive, reactionary, skills-based conceptions of literacy are both symptoms *and* causes of the unethical and problematic material conditions that merit our attention. If Shor is right about this, and I believe he is, then we must pay closer attention to how ambiguous and hasty characterizations of literacy *presuppose* the very arguments/conditions that lead to abolitionist polemics in the first place.

To be sure, much is at stake for English studies in rethinking literacy along the historical and theoretical lines posited by Shor's examination of basic writing, Street's ideological conception of literacy, and Graff's research on the perceived "crisis" and "decline" of literacy as well as the myths that make those perceptions possible. One way of rethinking literacy along these lines is by revisiting calls to abolish compulsory composition. Doing so emphasizes the complexity and contradictory nature of the relationship of attitudes about literacy to proposals for abolishing compulsory composition.

As I suggest in my introduction, proposals to abolish compulsory composition have been dismissed by scholars in composition because, in many cases, their arguments are perceived as merely elitist. Although this may be a valid assessment of the following studies, I hope to show how these elitist sentiments are inseparably intertwined with what the NLS terms as autonomous and strong theories of literacy. Histories by Connors and Russell overlook this aspect of these essays and represent abolitionists as resolute in their commitment both to the abolition of freshman English and liberal culture. However, as this next section asserts, these proposals are highly ambivalent and contradictory. They are far from resolute, and the elitist sensibilities associated with them are less significant than the vague and contradictory attitudes about literacy as well as the exaggerated expectations about the consequences of possessing literacy that underline their polemics.

THOMAS LOUNSBURY—"COMPULSORY COMPOSITION IN COLLEGES"

Undoubtedly, 1911 is a significant year for English studies and the compulsory composition debate. By the time Thomas Lounsbury made the first call for the abolition of composition in that year, first-year English as a university subject was over a century old (Bartholomae 1950). Robert Connors marks this time as a threshold moment, suggesting that by 1910 "most issues in composition methodology were decided, one way or another" (13). James Berlin also sees this period as key, noting in *Rhetoric and Reality: Writing Instruction in American Colleges, 1900–1985* that although the establishment of the Modern Language Association (MLA) in 1883 secured a place for English studies in the curriculum of higher education, it was the development of the National Council of Teachers of English (NCTE) in 1911 that signaled a commitment to theorizing and researching the teaching of writing for high school students. However, in the same year that pedagogical methodologies were coalescing around the development of professional organizations and some continuity and agreement in methodology in composition, one of the first indications of disagreement and dissatisfaction with compulsory composition emerged: *Harper's Monthly Magazine* published Thomas Lounsbury's article "Compulsory Composition in Colleges."

An Emeritus Professor of English at Yale University, Lounsbury worked in philology and linguistics and was one of the first (along with Edward A. Allen, William Mathews, and George Krapp) to question English instructors' "total acceptance of traditional rigid grammar" (Connors, *Composition-Rhetoric* 150). In *The Standard of Usage in English*, he opposes absolute conceptualizations of grammatical propriety and the writing handbooks that impose such rules on students, arguing that "in order to have a language become fixed, it is first necessary that those who speak it should become dead" (150). Indeed, Lounsbury's work on grammar, in part, helped to infuse a "descriptive spirit" into philological and pedagogical practices during the early 1900s (150). Such a disposition places Lounsbury in the company of specialists who questioned notions of grammar prescriptivism and also sought to reform teaching practices towards an end that conceptualized linguistics and language in a way that foreshadows modern attitudes about grammar and language. This orientation makes Lounsbury's proposal for abolishing composition worthy of closer consideration.

Lounsbury begins his proposal by suggesting that the problems of freshman composition cannot be conceived fully without empathy. "There is nothing so certain," he writes, "to warp the conclusions of the pure intellect working on this subject as actual experience" (866). Unfortunately, his thesis, which appears well into the article, is little help in determining his principal objections to compulsory composition. In what appears to be an attempt to consolidate his doubts about the course, he notes,

> Still, none the less am I thoroughly convinced that altogether undue importance is attached to exercises in English composition, especially compulsory exercises; that the benefits to be derived from the general practice in schools is vastly overrated; that the criticism of themes, even when it is fully competent, is in the majority of cases of little value to the recipient; that in a large number of instances the criticism is and must ever be more or less incompetent; and that when the corrections which are made are made inefficiently and unintelligently, as is too often the case, the results reached are distinctly more harmful than helpful. (869)

Although we appear to have, here, Lounsbury's reasons for a proposal to abolish compulsory composition, this line of reasoning is, in fact, only tangentially related to the themes, evidence, claims, and rationales marshaled on behalf of his position throughout his study. That is, the scope of Lounsbury's complaints about freshman English is so broad that it is not clear if abolishing compulsory composition is actually something that he sees as a solution or the problem. His position seems inconsistent, at times, even equivocal, and his ambivalence, I believe, is indicative of only a vague understanding of the purpose and value of literacy in compulsory composition.

For instance, we may find one source of Lounsbury's ambivalence in the attitudes he expresses about the value of literacy, its relationship to rhetoric, and its role in composition instruction and institutions of learning in general. In disputing the "delusive notion" that "institutions of learning have any monopoly of training in composition," Lounsbury responds with a question: "Why do men who have never had the advantage of any school training in composition so often express themselves with clearness, directness, and force?" For Lounsbury, the tribulations and successes of Ulysses Grant hold some answers to this question. "It is not probable that General Grant ever had much practice in writing in his youth," he notes; "What little he did have, it is more than probable he did not profit by. But participation in a mighty struggle, the ceaseless pressure of arduous duties and wearing responsibilities furnished him an intellectual training which it was not in the power of the schools to impart. Hence when he came to write his autobiography, he wrote it with a simplicity and consequent effectiveness which no mere drill in English could have wrought" (875).

This passage from Lounsbury is remarkable for several reasons. First, it is perhaps one of the clearest statements of what he finds to be inadequate about freshman English, namely, the drills and other repetitive exercises aimed toward teaching students to write themes. Clearly, Lounsbury finds such assignments to be inefficient and impractical. Second, Lounsbury's anecdote introduces and bolsters a claim that runs throughout his argument, that pain and misery felt through "participation in a mighty struggle" bring about the desired attributes that formal composition instruction only aspires to provide. We see this idea crop up throughout his study, but most notably in yet another reference to a famous American figure: Abraham Lincoln. Lounsbury notes:

> It is not likely that the direct instruction in composition he ever received took up much of his time, if indeed it took up any of it. But in his profession he found imposed upon him as a condition of success the necessity of clear thinking, with its usual accompaniment of clearness of expression. But the further education which produced the matchless simplicity and majesty of the brief Gettysburg oration was the outcome of the discipline of anxious days and sleepless nights, the never-ceasing pressure of the burden of care which waited upon the long agony of the Civil War. As a matter of fact, indeed, there is nothing like misery to improve the style." (875)

Here Lounsbury presents a tendency akin to what Mike Rose refers to as a "strong" theory of literacy. Lounsbury's claim is that misery, pain, anguish, and struggle bring about the acquisition of particular cognitive traits and the successful demonstration of "clearness of expression." For Lounsbury, Grant and Lincoln possessed clear thinking, style, and other desirable traits because they struggled through seemingly insurmountable experiences and achieved a "condition of success" in those situations. As such, they possessed the tenacity and willingness to endure various forms of "misery," and in doing so they gained style and clarity of thought and expression. Lounsbury's assertions are reminiscent of how some basic writers are sometimes misunderstood by institutions of learning and composition instructors more specifically. That is, composition students are sometimes seen as lacking the ability to think analytically and clearly about complex philosophical relationships. Because they are unable to demonstrate successfully these traits in academic conventions or other writing assignments, they are sometimes viewed as lazy or similar to cultures lacking literacy. Such understandings misrepresent the cognitive potential and capacities of basic writers as well as non-literate cultures, perpetuating "great divide" conceptions of literacy. The presence of such thinking in this proposal to abolish English is significant because it demonstrates a notable consequence of possessing a "strong" conception of literacy or exaggerated understandings of literacy's powers.

Some might argue that Lounsbury is not talking about literacy at all. Instead, Lounsbury simply wants students to gain experience, endure hard work, and achieve clarity in thought and expression. After all, by invoking abstractions like "clearness of expression," "matchless simplicity," and "style" he is actually (and perhaps unknowingly) discussing tenets of nineteenth-century Scottish rhetoric.[2] Lounsbury, however, is very clear about how he feels about rhetoric specifically, noting, "It has a value of its own; but it has not the kind of value which is often mistakenly claimed for it. For as grammar is nothing but the generalization of the facts of utterance, so rhetoric is nothing but the generalization of the facts of style" (875). On the one hand, the distinction between rhetoric and grammar that Lounsbury draws is clearly a move intended to anticipate rebuttals to his proposal. Given his complaints about freshman English, a reasonable response to Lounsbury would simply propose an alternative to theme-based writing pedagogy, perhaps something grounded specifically in rhetoric (and in many cases this is what happened in universities). On the other hand, when we examine his attacks on rhetoric more closely, we find that literacy and the ostensible consequences of possessing it are very much at play in his diatribe. He writes:

> I call to mind a young man who before beginning his Commencement oration went carefully through the whole of Whately's treatise on rhetoric as a preparatory exercise, and was much astounded to discover, after finishing it, that he could write no better than he did before. (875)

Lounsbury's proposal is indicative of an overly simplistic conception of human cognition. This perspective coupled with recurrent distinctions between rhetoric and grammar, oratory and writing, and the importance of pain and pleasure in the process of literacy acquisition demonstrate a quintessential characteristic of being caught in the literacy myth: According to Graff, "The point is that we are in the grips of the 'literacy myth.' We do not know precisely what we mean by literacy or what we expect individuals to achieve from their instruction in and possession of literacy" (*The Literacy Myth* 323). When we examine more closely the ways that Lounsbury articulates the aims and problems of freshman English in 1911, we find inconsistent understandings and definitions of literacy as well as unrealistic consequences of possessing it. When we treat these strong conceptualizations of literacy as evidence used to argue for the abolition of compulsory composition, it becomes clear that Lounsbury does not know precisely what he expects individuals to achieve from composition instruction.

It is easy to dismiss many of Lounsbury's claims, especially since so many of his musings on freshman composition are, on the level of tone, quite cynical and ironic. However, it is precisely Lounsbury's disposition that caught the attention of Thomas Percival Beyer in 1912 when he published his response to Lounsbury in *The Educational Review*. Appearing in the "Discussion" section and titled, "Anent Compulsory Composition in Colleges," Beyer is clearly conflicted about Lounsbury's proposal. On the one hand, he finds it "the most readable essay on a technical and polemic theme that I have seen in a long while" (77). Furthermore, Beyer is "grateful to Professor Lounsbury" for putting the "classic argument against English in the most cogent way possible" (84). Yet, he objects to the central assumptions driving the essay and the position in which those assumptions put teachers of composition. It is important to examine Beyer's response to Lounsbury because even though he takes issue with most of Lounsbury's assertions, the two scholars share much in common when it comes to the assumptions they make about the powers and place of literacy in compulsory composition.

Beyer is suspicious of theme-based pedagogies, agreeing with Lounsbury that drills in compulsory composition fail in their aims of creating literary geniuses—he calls such assignments "illogical and absurd" (84). However, he questions Lounsbury's assumption that colleges of the time "retain freshman composition in the required list because they still see the vision of Utopia populated by a nation of Carlyles, Goethes, and Tolstois" (78). He asserts that he has never "heard of a college that set out to produce a race of literary artists." On the contrary, he knows "of a few, at all events, that are striving to send out men—just men, and perhaps, a leaven of women" (78). Indeed, Beyer's statement points to divergent attitudes about the aims of freshman English as well as opposing understandings of the purposes of universities at this time. However, what he proposes as a solution to the dilemma presented by freshman English is not so different from the ambivalence and assumptions driving Lounsbury's proposal.

In the end, Beyer seems dismayed by Lounsbury's critiques and resents the implications of his article. "Since no honest man could continue to draw a salary for wasteful work," he writes, "the dilemma presents itself that I am either a knave or a fool. I am a fool if I believe in my work; I am a knave if I do not, in which case I think I am a greater fool than ever for not getting out of it" (84). Despite such feelings he concludes that "composition taught in a sensible normal way does not bore the average freshman, and does contribute to the art of living" (84). For Beyer, a "sensible" and "normal" approach to composition instruction is less systematic, opposed to the "state of extreme mental busy-ness" imposed by theme writing.[3]

> Start with description. Teach observation a few weeks, hammer home just about three principles: fidelity to nature, selection of detail, and the value of verbs and words denoting action as well as specific instead of generic terms. Then send him out to describe the people on the street-cars, a football scrimmage, a scene in a play, the chatter of blackbirds in the wild rice, or how it feels to swim or row or race, and I defy the dullest teacher in Christendom to prevent a freshman from sitting up and taking notice. Later he can find delight in narrating some of his own thrilling experiences, or constructing a complication about a young man, his duty, and his sweetheart; and, finally, he can even be induced to tell what he thinks about "College spirit" or "Eligibility rules in athletics." (83)

Although this approach, according to Beyer, realizes one aim of freshman English—to teach students "to describe a person, a picture, a view, with a fair degree of accuracy, and even present a coherent reason for the particular faith that may be within him" (83)—this alone is not enough. What college students need "more than anything else" are "Between-Times" (86)—the "occasional half-hour of real loafing, and inviting the soul." However, according to Beyer, there are limits to this loafing. If students write nothing, "the soul that he gets glimmerings of will remain a spiritual embryo. It will never be fixed, and he will never gain confidence in it" (86). Thus, in one sense, freshman English and the requisite drills and tasks that constitute the course are the problem: "With a daily theme prodding him, he can never wait for an idea, but writes drivel and grows cynical" (86). But at the same time, freshman English is the solution because without the course students remain intellectually and spiritually undeveloped.

Even though Lounsbury and Beyer are on opposite sides of the abolition debate—Lounsbury opposes the requirement and Beyer seems to desire reforming the teaching of composition—both of their arguments are sustained by an abiding belief in the power of literacy to bring about profound cognitive and spiritual transformations. Their exchange highlights the ways in which ambiguous definitions of literacy and exaggerated expectations of possessing it motivate proposals both for and against compulsory composition. Taken together, these essays are an early example of how the debate over compulsory composition involves much more than disagreements over pedagogy or the aptitude of students and instructors. From the perspective of the NLS, we may understand the attitudes about literacy that underline these studies as linked to a tradition of characterizing literacy in a way that exaggerates its powers. This move is based on simplistic assumptions not only of human cognition but also of the role of cognition in the relationship of literacy to teaching, learning, and educational reforms. In addition to demonstrating that myths of literacy are ever-present in the defining positions of the abolition debate, Lounsbury and Beyer are particularly interesting because of how they reflect pressures brought on by the trend toward academic specialization and other educational reforms of their time.

By 1911, the year in which Lounsbury published his essay on freshman English, higher education was entering a time marked by the rise of academic hierarchies, professional associations, unprecedented growth, and other consequences of academic specialization. Although compulsory composition was the focal point of many scholars' antipathy during this time, the impact of academic specialization underscored and complicated attempts to bring about lasting reform and change in the humanities more generally, not simply in the teaching of freshman English. The historical context surrounding Lounsbury's argument must be considered alongside the central arguments of his proposal. In this next section, I sketch a brief history of academic specialization with Lounsbury's proposal in mind. I do this to demonstrate that in the case of calls to abolish compulsory composition, exaggerated expectations of literacy's powers and other myths of literacy overlap with specific institutional pressures and educational reforms from the history of higher education.

CHARACTERISTICS AND CONSEQUENCES OF ACADEMIC SPECIALIZATION

The abolition debate and the proposals that constitute this conversation are compelling in part because they are often spirited in tone and grandiose in scope. However, twenty years before Lounsbury's study, we find proposals for larger educational reform that dwarf the implications of calls to abolish compulsory freshman English. For example, in 1891, "Pitchfork Ben" Tillman, a gubernatorial candidate locked in a spirited campaign, wanted more than the abolition of the teaching of freshman English (Veysey 15). As part of his plan to get elected, Tillman promised to abolish the entire

University of South Carolina. Of this time, Laurence Veysey notes, "It was in such an unfriendly climate as this that the American university initially had to make its way" (15). What made the climate particularly interesting for composition was something far more complex than the whims of policy makers. John C. Brereton notes in *The Origins of Composition Studies in the American College, 1875–1925* that several factors stand out as principal influences on the development of universities at the turn of the century.[4] However, it is the period of academic specialization (1870–1920) that was the most consequential pressure shaping the development of freshman composition as well as the critiques of the course.

The trend toward academic specialization was a series of transinstitutional reforms that led to an increase in the variety of subjects and the dividing of departments into an extensive selection of fields and subdepartments. In *The Emergence of the American University*, Laurence Veysey' observes most strikingly that this period was marked by considerable confusion, variety, and divergent attitudes about the perceived benefits and consequences of specialization.[5] Consequently, "a distinct and 'cultivated elite' of professors, schoolmasters, authors, clergymen, and others remain isolated from mainstream American life" (51–52). We may understand Lounsbury as one of these "cultivated elites" who seems agitated by the way that academic specialization has attenuated the influence of literary approaches in the teaching of composition. Furthermore, that Lounsbury's proposal to abolish compulsory composition appeared in *Harper's Monthly Magazine* rather than one of the many academic journals emerging at this time is significant. I believe that this is evidence of both his resistance to the trend toward academic specialization as well as his need to articulate his frustrations with freshman English to a wider, more mainstream audience. After all, although many of his colleagues (like Beyer) disagreed with aspects of his proposal to abolish compulsory composition, the *Harper's* audience may well have shared something in common with Lounsbury: namely, an abiding belief in the literacy myth.

During the early stages of academic specialization, the direction, purpose, and ostensible function and nature of American higher education was determined by conflicts "first along the lines of competing academic goals, then over questions of academic command" (Veysey viii). As such, when Veysey remarks on the "difficult times" from which the American university emerges, he refers to a period marred by confusion and a diversity of perspectives and experiences. As universities transformed in response to the pressure to become more intellectually segmented, writing instruction became "confined to well-defined courses" (Brereton 9). In Lounsbury's eyes, because freshman English emerges from this period of academic specialization, it was a distinctly "modern" consequence of educational reform. "Work of the sort now implied by it," he writes, "was then a novelty in American institutions of learning. The attention at present paid to English language and literature is not only modern, it is late modern. Knowledge of it as a requirement for entrance is even more modern" (866). It is revealing that for Lounsbury modernity becomes a matter of degree when it comes to the requirement of freshman English (it is not just modern but "more modern"). Just as important, however, is the fact that Lounsbury shifts his focus away from criticisms about how English is being taught to whether it should be taught at all. His reference to a time when such work is a "novelty" is clearly an attempt at broadening the scope of his argument to account for a history that he feels is being forgotten. This history is the story of English studies' struggle to gain respect and prestige—to become a discipline in the new university.

Nowhere in its history is the attempt at gaining institutional prestige and respect more clear than in English departments' commitments to the precepts of philology. To put it bluntly, English had a difficult time gaining a respected place in the research university. Several notable histories of English attest to this fact. Arthur Applebee's *Tradition and Reform in the Teaching of English: A History* and Gerald Graff's *Professing Literature: An Institutional History* both speak to the challenges that English faced and the ways that philology simultaneously attenuated and magnified the project of gaining disciplinary status. Admittedly, this issue is well-traveled ground, especially in the most cited histories of higher education and English studies.[6] However, in the context of this study, exploring the role of philology in the rise of English departments provides a greater stage for my discussion of literacy. By this, I mean, regardless of whether scholars argue for or against compulsory composition, literacy functions as an aim in both approaches. I emphasize the history of philology here because it is a necessary part of exploring how particular theoretical commitments in the history of English have helped to construct literacy as an aim, end, and foundation for the discipline.

PURSUING PRESTIGE: PHILOLOGY AND THE RISE OF THE DEPARTMENT OF ENGLISH

In addressing the influence of philology in the formation of English departments, historians have emphasized several aspects of this process. In *Professing Literature*, Gerald Graff sees the rise of philology and the "professionalization" of the discipline of English as inextricably linked. He notes, "the advance guard of professionalization was a German-trained cadre of scholarly 'investigators,' who promoted the idea of scientific research and the philological study of the modern languages" (55). The importance and rapidity of the move to align the aims of English with scientific research cannot be understated when considering philology's impact on the field. According to Graff, as early as the first meeting of the Modern Language Association, H. C. G. Brandt (a Hamilton College Professor of German) proclaims "our department *is* a science, and . . . its teaching must be carried on accordingly" (qtd. in Graff 68). Motivating Brandt was a concern that if teachers of language failed to understand their departments as science, that "any body" would feel they could teach English (68). "By introducing scientific methods," Brandt asserts, "we shall show before very long that every body cannot [teach English], that the teacher must be as specially and as scientifically trained for his work in our department as well as in any other" (qtd. in Graff 68). Brandt's statements underscore the ways that the scientific underpinnings of philology function to dignify the work of English at this time.

Writing in "Secularization and Sacralization: Speculations on Some Religious Origins of the Secular Humanities Curriculum, 1850–1900," James Turner explains that philology was cultivated in Germany in the eighteenth century and transplanted to the English-speaking world in the early nineteenth. Providing a "powerful paradigm of knowledge well into the second half of the century," philology led to a unique approach to college instruction, "belonging to neither the antebellum classical curriculum nor the twentieth-century liberal arts" (83). What is remarkable about the impact of philology on English instruction, despite arguments to the contrary, is the extent to which this theoretical commitment traversed multiple subdisciplines simultaneously. In "Literary Study and the Modern System of the Disciplines," John Guillory notes that by the 1890s four disciplinary practices—philology, composition, belles lettres, and literary history—exist simultaneously in departments of English (35). And while an overarching influence of the formation of English studies "was driven by the development of a principle of scientificity" owing primarily to precepts of philology, this "arrangement," as Guillory notes, "did not prevail in the long term" (35).

Ultimately, because philology failed to figure inquiry into literature on scientific grounds, it paradoxically "weakened its claim to scientificity" (36). Moreover, philology's predicament was compounded by the conditions and consequences of academic specialization, resulting in a more limited "definition of philology as a study of language" (Applebee 26). This narrowed scope and understanding of its aims coupled with increasingly "lofty goals" and "pedantic textual criticism" led, in part, to the somewhat negative image that it possesses today (26). In many ways, the failure of philology holds the most pressing implications for this study. Gerald Graff reminds us that philology "proved a dismal failure only in relation to expectations that few of its early proponents were attempting to meet" (68). What survived of philology was a "larger cultural vision," a way of thinking about language and the university that aspired to reconcile seemingly incompatible directions for teaching and research within English departments. It met a desire, a "nostalgia for the past, especially the European past and the Middle Ages," but it also satisfied a need for "facts, for accuracy, for the imitation of the 'scientific method' which had acquired overwhelming prestige" (Wellek qtd. in Graff 68). Whereas the rise of philology is evidence of the distinct ways in which departments like English undergo a process of intellectual segmentation during this period, it is important to remember—as Veysey discusses—that behind the conflict of philology's humanistic and positivistic impulses, a process of bureaucratization and standardization also accompanies academic specialization. This aspect of specialization is also inextricably linked with the fiscal health and unprecedented growth of universities at the turn of the twentieth century.

By 1911, consequences of academic specialization were becoming impossible for professors like Lounsbury to ignore, especially with respect to the number of students attending university (and his own composition class) as well as the amount of money flowing through his institution. In the *Organization of Knowledge in Modern America, 1860–1920*, Alexandra Oleson and John Voss report that in 1899 the thirty-four largest gifts pledged to public causes totaled $80 million; of that amount, more than $55 million was given to institutions of higher learning, more than $5 million to libraries, and almost $3 million to museums (xi). Meanwhile, according to the authors, the number of undergraduates in American universities increased from 52,300 in 1870 to 156,800 in 1890; 237,600 in 1900; and 597,900 in 1920 (xii). The type of university (in the nature of its work and in its students' demographics) that Lounsbury inhabited in 1911 was almost unrecognizable in comparison to the university where he began teaching 25 years before he made his proposal to abolish compulsory composition. Certainly, the changes he witnessed in universities influenced his decision to call for the abolition of compulsory composition. However, Lounsbury's article is highly ambivalent and conflicted about whether abolishing compulsory composition addresses the problem of providing adequate writing instruction for growing numbers of students. This ambivalence may be symptomatic of the fact that support for the trend toward specialization was waning in the 1910s and 1920s. In fact, in *The Making of the Modern University: Intellectual Transformation and The Marginalization of Morality*, Julie A. Reuben asserts that although surveys of college and university presidents in 1901 characterize the elective system as a "fixture" in colleges, by 1920 the trend seemed to reverse (231). Searching for ways to articulate the relevance of their work and to establish some sense of coherence and continuity in curriculums, some professors and administrators in the early 1920s became highly critical of specialization. In its place "liberal culture" becomes, as James Turner calls it, the "new buzzword of undergraduate general education" (79). In the abolitionist argument of Oscar James Campbell, we find evidence of the pressures imposed both by the trend toward specialization and by liberal culture on general education courses like freshman composition.

OSCAR JAMES CAMPBELL— THE FAILURE OF FRESHMAN ENGLISH

Unlike Lounsbury's "Compulsory College Composition," which was published in *Harper's Magazine* and taken seriously enough to spark a rebuttal from Beyer in the *Educational Review* in 1912, Oscar James Campbell's proposal was met only with reformist arguments and dissent (Connors 8–9).[7] Despite such criticism, Campbell's "The Failure of Freshman English" is one of the few proposals discussed by all existing histories of the abolition debate, as well as by most respected histories of composition. In this section, I discuss aspects of Campbell's study that have been overlooked by historians of writing instruction. In particular, I show how Campbell's essay depends on what Ruth Finnegan and others from the NLS describe as a "Great Divide" conception of literacy. As I discussed in the first part of this chapter, "great divide" conceptions of literacy are indicative of a theoretical assumption about learning that inaccurately elevates those possessing literacy to positions of dominance over those that do not. By attending to the role of Campbell's attitude about literacy, we understand better how the rhetoric of abolitionism depends on generalizations that accompany the literacy myth.

Campbell is a compelling figure for historians of composition and the abolition debate because of his use of metaphor and the hostility of his rhetoric. He begins his tirade on freshman English by comparing compulsory composition to a monster, specifically a "Frankenstein" which was created by a former colleague, Barrett Wendell, and has gone awry. He chides the course for forcing "teachers of English to attempt what they know is impossible and [building] up false ideas and false hopes of the educational process which vitiates undergraduate work in almost the entire curriculum" (178). As contemporary as his assessment might sound to us, such sentiments should not be confused with progressive understandings of literacy; in fact, more than any other proposal to abolish freshman English, Campbell's study is marked by inconsistent and contradictory conceptions of literacy. For example, Campbell asserts, "Only through the books of ages remote from his own can an individual completely emancipate himself from the provinciality of time and place" (183). Which is to say, without "works of literature" in the tradition of liberal culture, students are like primitive creatures, unable to gain the critical distance and cognitive skills to objectively understand their position in time and space. In this same vein, Campbell is convinced that literature—not compulsory composition (and the sophisticated levels of literacy that literature makes possible)—leads to extraordinary consequences. "Without some modicum of thinking," he explains, "one cannot write at all, and it is emphatically true that one cannot ever write any better than he can think" (179). To be sure, Campbell's statement is indicative of a "great divide" conception of literacy in which reductive epistemological assumptions related to the perceived consequences of being literate inform his position on compulsory composition. However, even more important to note, are the ways Campbell's claims about the relationship between thinking and writing are symptomatic of a model of language acquisition and production, a model that situates literacy as an independent variable in that process. After all, Campbell is not only suggesting that freshman English students are illiterate—or "without letters" (Rose, "The Language of Exclusion" 597); in his view, they are also without minds.

However, unlike Lounsbury, Campbell's opposition to the requirement is not completely supported by what Brian Street and others from the NLS have described as strong theories of literacy that subscribe to an autonomous model. In fact, at times, Campbell seems to question specifically the pedagogical effectiveness of instruction based on restricted conceptions of literacy. For instance, in discussing the methods employed by composition courses of the time he notes, "The existence of the course and the methods it habitually employs are based on the fallacious notion that good writing is a *Ding an Sich*, a separate independent technique. That is, that it can be engendered and grown in a kind of intellectual vacuum" (178). In a way, Campbell sees the aims of composition courses as varying from moment to moment; they cannot be defined and achieved in a vacuum or apart from other contexts. He supports this position further by drawing on an analogy intended to demonstrate the flawed thinking behind prevailing approaches to composition at the time. "If the proponents of this course have any philosophy," he writes, "it is that one learns to write sentences as one learns to play scales on the piano and for the same purpose" (178). What Campbell means by this is that it is assumed if a piano student masters particular skills in both the major and minor scales, s/he may successfully and equally apply such skills to "the successful rendition of a Beethoven sonata or of a Franz Liszt rhapsody" (178). Campbell concedes that his "music analogy is very imperfect" (178) but believes that this thinking is behind compulsory composition instruction at the time. More specifically, Campbell senses that composition instructors treat "words, phrases, and sentences" as if they are notes on a scale that correspond to a keyboard, as if language itself is "external to the process of playing anything and independent of it" (178). Although Campbell fails to offer solutions to this problem specifically, he does speculate as to why such instruction continues, and he lays blame not on composition instructors or students, but on administrators and professors in other departments.

This assertion marks a curious shift in tone in Campbell's essay. Up to this point, Campbell's complaints about compulsory composition are not directed at any person in particular. Instead, he seems only interested in aspects of the course that support his claims regarding its ineffectiveness and inefficiency. However, when he speculates about how and why universities have allowed the situation with compulsory composition to continue so inefficiently and for so long, he explains,

> Our students, then, do not take seriously our pedagogic pretensions, but the administrators of the universities and the professors in other departments than our own most emphatically do. Presidents and deans continue to say by word of mouth, and by word of pen, that the principal business of an English department is to teach all the students in a university how to write well. Universities spend vast sums of money on that service; in fact, so much that the budget of the English department is commonly about twice as large as that of any other department in the undergraduate college. It is natural then that the administration believes that it is entitled to much more positive results than it is obtaining. We should not be surprised that it keeps insisting that the English department must discover new and better methods of doing its main job. (180)

Unlike Lounsbury's proposal, in which institutional pressures are latent and tangentially related to his argument, Campbell responds directly to pressures from the administrative order of universities. This passage highlights specifically the ways that assumptions about the purpose and powers of literacy overlap with administrative pressures. Campbell's proposal is motivated largely by exaggerated understandings of literacy's powers, and he perceives that such attitudes prevail in administrative circles as well. However, and most importantly, he objects to these attitudes if they originate from deans and university presidents. What lies at the heart of the debate over compulsory composition in Campbell's argument is not the compulsory nature of the course or its pedagogical methods. Instead, competing attitudes about literacy are actually motivating this conflict, and the confusion surrounding these definitions, attitudes, and characterizations grows out of competing visions of the purposes of universities altogether.

Many scholars, like David R. Russell, would argue that Campbell's latent attitudes about literacy and the institutional contexts complicating his position are less relevant than his romantic commitments to liberal culture.[8] In "Romantics on Writing: Liberal Culture and the Abolition of Composition Courses" Russell contends that "arguments used to attack" (132) compulsory composition are consistent with the guiding precepts of liberal culture specifically (which I touch on briefly in the next section). Although I concede that Campbell's investment in the Arnoldian ideal of the "well-rounded man" informs his position on compulsory composition, I believe that his explicit statement about and irritation with the expectations of "the administration" and "professors in other departments" hold important implications for understanding how the Great Debate is perpetuated.

Campbell shows us that the engine of the debate over compulsory composition is yet another myth. Mike Rose calls this the "myth of transience," or the persistent belief "in the American university that if we can just do x or y, the problem will be solved—in five years, ten years, or a generation—and higher education will be able to return to its real work" ("The Language of Exclusion" 599). Rose claims the myth is a complete fiction, but a potentially useful one with significant implications. In one sense, the myth of transience provides hope, as every generation of scholars' problems are new to those who tangle with them, and when faced with problems, people must believe that a solution exists (600). On the other hand, the myth of transience—much like Graff's understanding of the literacy myth—tends to obscure history, especially those aspects of the history of higher education that are complex, dynamic in nature, and not easily defined or understood (600). Yet, despite its tendency to blind scholars to "historical reality," the myth of transience persists. "Like any golden age or utopian myth," Rose writes, "the myth of transience assures its believers that the past was better or that the future will be" (600).[9] When considered in the context of Campbell's situation, where ongoing debates between scholars and administrators seem defined by differences over the effectiveness of composition, we find the myth of transience both obfuscating the actual problems prolonging the debate—competing definitions of literacy—and also temporarily reconciling these seemingly incompatible positions. In other words, this myth simultaneously elides attitudes about literacy *and* temporarily resolves the confusion that stems from competing visions for compulsory composition. From this perspective we may understand the Great Debate as sustained not by arguments over composition's effectiveness (nor quibbles over which pedagogical approach is the best) but by competing attitudes about the nature of literacy—characterizations and attitudes that, as I have shown in my discussion of Campbell, are made latent by confiding simultaneously in Rose's myth of transience and Graff's literacy myth.

It should not come as a surprise, then, that like Lounsbury, Campbell never articulates specifically how he defines literacy. However, when we examine more closely what Campbell believes is ultimately at stake in the mission of universities, a more precise definition of the incentives of literacy becomes evident. "It is undoubtedly trite," he asserts, "to say that the success of a democratic state depends upon the sort of life that is lived by the individuals who compose it" (183). Furthermore, these individuals must be "self-reliant" yet "sensitive to the needs of other individuals," especially when it comes to assessing "the impact of their own personalities" on others. For Campbell, only one type of literacy possesses the power to cultivate the kind of citizens that can sustain his vision of a successful democracy. David Barton calls this "the literary view of literacy" (168). Of its powers Campbell notes, "Literature cultivates and sharpens this sensitivity by enabling the individual to share, and thus to understand, a great variety of human experiences" (183). According to Campbell, "every work of literature" is an "essential part of the living tissue of the life of every age." And only through this type of literacy or "the books of the ages remote from his own can an individual completely emancipate himself from the provinciality of time and place" (183).

Although Campbell occasionally expresses notions that question restricted conceptions of literacy, his literary view of literacy clearly subscribes to great divide conceptions. Without great books, students remain tied to the present, unable to gain the cognitive faculties to distance themselves from the moment; according to this theory of literacy, they forever lack the interpretive skills and perspective necessary to deal with abstract ideals and philosophical problems in sophisticated ways. Thus—and despite Campbell's many complaints directed toward the shortcomings of theme-based pedagogies—the problems of compulsory composition may be boiled down to a course that is not cultivating the tastes and behaviors that literature provides. In this way, Campbell's literary view of literacy was, on the one hand, a solution to the ostensible shortcomings of compulsory composition. Yet, because this view of literacy was not translating into the type of classroom practices that would meet administrator's expectations, it was also the problem.

Other significant contradictions are apparent in this scenario. Campbell's essay also shows how incongruent great divide and literary views of literacy can be with the exaggerated, generalized, and universalized expectations of myths of literacy that often inform institutional and administrative pressures. Certainly, as my reading of Campbell demonstrates, competing and contradictory characterizations of literacy complicate efforts to evaluate the aims and effectiveness of freshman English. However, it is also important to remember that structures of authority and power relations among faculty and administrators are also at stake in the rhetoric of abolitionism. We get some sense of these pressures when we examine further Campbell's tone and his concerns about the working conditions of composition instructors.

David Russell contends that even though the "rhetorical contexts differ" between Lounsbury and Campbell, the "rhetorical strategies" of the proposals are essentially the same. According to Russell, Campbell, like Lounsbury, uses irony as a trope to rally his audience around the "cardinal principle of Romanticism" and liberal culture (Russell 135). Certainly, Campbell's article contains moments of sarcasm.[10] But irony and sarcasm are not the predominant traits of this prolonged critique of compulsory composition. On the contrary, Campbell's proposal is remarkable for another, equally compelling response: namely, his concerns over the teaching conditions for instructors of freshman English.

> But, for all that, crowds of young men and women have been lured into the teaching of English by the great numbers of positions annually open at the bottom of the heap, and there they stick, contaminating one another with their discouragement and rebellion. No wonder they are now organizing, as other proletariats the world over are organizing, to assert and foster their class interests. In almost every institution in which there is a chapter of the teacher's union, instructors in English form its central core. (181–182)

Campbell's proposal is interesting because it is a spirited polemic and occasionally sarcastic, but here, he is also speaking candidly about the challenges of composition instruction at a particular moment. In this passage, Campbell remarks on the exploitative working conditions that many composition instructors experienced leading up to this period. Campbell would have been especially attuned to such conditions and feedback because, just four years earlier, he held a position of influence during a time in which the profession was experiencing a "proliferation of debates" (Roemer et al. 380). In "Reframing the Great Debate on First-Year Writing," Marjorie Roemer, Lucille M. Schultz, and Russel K. Durst report that because of "strong divisions among college English instructors" in the 1930s, the NCTE formed a committee to issue a report on the state of college English. Campbell presided over that committee, and according to the authors "he [Campbell] argued strongly against the first-year course in a way that is very consistent with previous abolitionist arguments" (380). This may be true, but more interesting is that Campbell specifically articulates in the report the constraints and demands of his cultural moment, and he does so in a way that never happens in his proposal to abolish freshman English. This is important to note because contemporary receptions of Campbell's abolitionist proposal cast him as a literary elitist frustrated by the way that composition attenuates the "usefulness of literary education" (Connors 285). And yet, a closer look at the perspective emerging in the following report indicates that Campbell's position was much more complex. In *The Teaching of College English* he notes:

> Adequate mastery of the English language, however, should mean much more than the attainment of mere correctness and literate respectability. It should imply effective communication of ideas. Many cooperative enterprises essential to the existence of a sound social organization are dependent on a fairly wide diffusion of this ability, particularly among our social and political leaders. President Roosevelt's skill in explaining to the entire nation the policies and actions of the government, particularly in the banking crisis of 1933, created overnight a new attitude toward our entire economic structure. This, in turn, has contributed largely to its safety and to the revival of its orderly operation. (7)

Certainly, when we proceed beyond the introduction, we find the reductive reasoning and elitist rationales that typify criticisms of compulsory composition during this time (and perhaps even today). However, in this passage, for a brief moment, Campbell's framing of how he understands pressures brought on by the Great Depression and other social developments give us reason to look beyond existing assessments of his role in the debate. Considering these social and economic contexts alongside the latent attitudes about literacy in his proposal to abolish composition lends perspective and provides greater understanding of the complex pressures that have helped to shape the abolition debate more generally.

For instance, let us return to Campbell's "The Failure of Freshman English," where he predicts that teachers of composition would continue to organize and protest the unfair working conditions and drudgery of freshman English as, he writes, "other proletariats the world over are organizing" (182). As problematic as his comparison is, in noting that such dissatisfaction and pressure is coming from all over the world, not simply from English departments or universities, Campbell underscores the ways in which many pro-abolitionist proposals are responding to and using to their advantage various cultural, social, and economic pressures. In Campbell's case, he seems to suggest that if composition is not abolished, the "crowds of young men and women" who have been "lured into the teaching of English" will organize and revolt with the intention of overthrowing the "Freshman English machine" (181) . . . or so he seems to hope.

It would be easy, I think, to dismiss such statements as hyperbolic—which may be one reason scholars have ignored this aspect of Campbell's study—but from the perspective of the New Literacy Studies, we may read Campbell's predictions and concerns with the material conditions of composition in a new light. Above all, Campbell's statements indicate that his position, like Lounsbury's, is significantly more complex than once thought, and as I argue, this added dimension and nuance may be traced to Campbell's latent attitudes about and characterizations of literacy specifically. In a sense, Campbell's hopes for literacy to span the spectrum of "expectations of what it means to read and write, and what might follow from those practices attitudinaly, cognitively, individually, and collectively" (Graff, "The Literacy Myth at Thirty" 639). Such expectations, as Graff reminds us, are intimately connected to "imprecise, yet progressively grander conceptions" (639) of what literacy means to us. For Campbell, it is precisely grand conceptions that have lured English teachers to the "Freshman English machine." "They (composition instructors) want to be raised out of the drudgery," Campbell writes, "of marking futilely conceived and futilely executed exercises in words, words, words. Their work, they realize, has no relation whatever to the subject to which, in hopeful youth, they resolved to dedicate their lives" (182). In the end, then, Campbell's position on compulsory composition is motivated by the imprecise, and to be sure, highly varied hopes of instructors, aspirations which have been dashed by the drudgery of teaching composition—hopes that remain inextricably linked with the expectations they associate with attaining literacy. Ultimately, Campbell's suggestion is to abolish compulsory composition in order to embrace the "legitmate duties and prized opportunities" (185) that accompany a curriculum devoted to "English literature" (182). More "words, words, words," indeed, but only the kind that adhere to his great divide conception of literacy. More words that demonstrate a one to one relationship between conception and execution. More words that support a strong theory of literacy that situates the act of reading and writing as a solitary activity—as an independent variable in the composing process of freshman students.

The following chapter explicates arguments that touch on, among other critical issues, the tendency to conceive of literacy as an independent and neutral variable in cognition and communication. However, unlike Lounsbury and Campbell, the next section of *The Lure of Literacy* takes up studies that have been overlooked in existing histories of the abolition debate. As I have shown, calls for the abolition of compulsory composition correspond with particular institutional sea-changes, specifically educational reforms like the trend toward academic specialization and, to some extent, the rise and fall of philology and liberal culture. Early calls like Thomas Lounsbury's and Oscar James Campbell's should be rhetorically situated with an eye toward latent characterizations of literacy, as I have done. In doing so, significant intersections between the rhetoric of these arguments and the myths of literacy that sustain them become evident. Likewise, in examining the following overlooked proposals through the lens of the New Literacy Studies, we again find that relative pressures to both abolish and maintain the requirement of freshman English are based on exaggerated understandings of literacy's powers. Furthermore, by supplementing existing histories of the debate with voices that have been left out, the following chapter aims to provide a more complete picture of the debate over the aims and effectiveness of compulsory composition. My argument is that an important part of providing this more complete history must involve making more legible the persistent and tenacious attitudes about literacy that function as both solutions to the problems of compulsory composition and perpetuating factors in the debate itself.

TWO

THE SPHINX RIDDLE OF FRESHMAN ENGLISH

Examining Continuities of Literacy in the Great Debate

> What we know as Freshman English has all the earmarks of a makeshift, a temporary device. When our educational experts have disposed of other things, they will at last turn seriously to the matter of training in the use of English, and the course which now is virtually a mere Sphinx riddle defying solution will disappear altogether or will take a natural and effective place in a rationally conceived and thoroughly organized program of education in the mother-tongue. When that time comes, as ultimately we must believe it will, the present intricately contrived machinery of our courses in Freshman English will be thought of with curiosity and with compassion.
>
> —Frederick A. Manchester, May 1917

Despite numerous examinations of the abolition debate, many voices, like Frederick A. Manchester's, have been left out. One aim of this chapter is to supplement existing histories of the abolition debate—to incorporate overlooked voices of both abolitionism *and* reform to provide a more complete understanding of the debate over the compulsory requirement. E. A. Thurber's "Composition in Our Colleges" (1915) argues for more relevant methods of freshman English instruction. His study is evidence of the ways that the consequences of academic specialization extend well beyond the temporal boundaries historians of education have set for this period. Frederick A. Manchester's essays "Freshman English Once More" and "Freshman English Once More—Concluded" (1917) proceed along similar lines, but pose the question as to whether the "problems" of freshman English defy solution altogether. Responding to the economic and educational challenges of his time, Paulus Lange's "What Price English?" (1938) demonstrates how foregrounding the literacy myth in appeals to crisis leads to exaggerated expectations for literacy and freshman English. His solution, like Thurber and Manchester, is to pass on the burden of literacy instruction to high schools. Taken together, these studies demonstrate that the "Sphinx riddle" of freshman English is made even more perplexing by the attitudes about literacy that they share in common.

The approach I take in this chapter is similar to Harvey J. Graff's on the history of literacy in *The Legacies of Literacy: Continuities and Contradictions in Western Culture and Society*. One aim of his project is to emphasize continuities and contradictions with respect to the place of literacy in the history of Western culture and society (8). The language of continuity, he notes, is useful when discussing literacy because the circumstances surrounding it have involved gradual changes over time. "Concepts of continuity," he writes, "involve comparisons over time, as well as awareness of the need to determine the relationship between elements of change and continuity simultaneously operating in any historical moment or situation" (8). Graff's study employs the language of continuity to consider overlooked but profound similarities in various social and economic contexts as well as rates of literacy, institutional structures of schooling, and the "practical and symbolic uses of literacy" (8). Employing the language of continuity in my examination of the abolition debate allows me to challenge further the tendency to conceive of the abolition debate in terms of change and revolution. Similarly, and as Graff notes, "The history of literacy is typically conceived and written in terms of *change*. The assumption is that literacy, development, growth, and progress are inseparably linked" (8). As such, the legacies of literacy—the series of continuities that constitute the history of literacy—comprise not only the overlooked voices in the debate that I examine in this chapter, but also the existing histories of the debate that have left them out.

OVERLOOKED VOICES AND CONTINUITIES IN THE ABOLITION DEBATE

Published in *The English Journal* in 1915, E. A. Thurber's "Composition in Our Colleges" begins by celebrating Lounsbury's proposal for abolition, which appeared in *Harper's* four years earlier. Similar to other proposals of the time, it is a sarcastic essay that is dismissive of composition instruction more generally. However, unlike Lounsbury, Thurber offers a solution to the problem of freshman English; he proposes that the responsibility of composition instruction should fall to all disciplines that constitute universities, not simply English departments. More pragmatic and less polemical than Lounsbury, Thurber sees his proposal as an extension of the claims of previous criticisms of compulsory composition, as in his introduction, he notes:

> And here is where the band begins to play, where Professor Lounsbury, in his article in *Harper's* some two or three years ago, struck for many a harsh and unwelcome note. The problem, to be sure, is vexing and diverse; when you have broken through a man's center, you have always turned his flank. It is the flank movements in this discussion that prolong the warfare. (9)

Thurber's appropriation of military rhetoric is revealing, and I believe we may read it as a symptom of the impact of Lounsbury's study on prevailing thinking about compulsory composition. Thurber states that Lounsbury "struck for many a harsh and unwelcome note"; we know from Connors that Lounsbury's article "was not followed up in Harper's" (8), and although it is true that Lounsbury's "Compulsory Composition in Colleges" provoked a discussion in the *Educational Review* in 1913, his argument, as I noted in chapter 1, was more notorious than consequential. Given what we know about the reception of Lounsbury's proposal, what we find in Thurber's introduction is, I believe, an attempt at enhancing the impact of Lounsbury's overall argument. By suggesting that abolitionists like Lounsbury "have broken through" and provoked a defensive response (when, in fact, he has not), Thurber is positioning himself for a more strategic attack on compulsory composition. To be sure, his antipathy for freshman English is more focused and specific than his predecessors, as his efforts are directed specifically toward the pedagogical apparatus and perceived need for freshman English.

More provocative than his use of military rhetoric (or the more strategic levels on which his study operates), is his interest in the role of literacy as a learning outcome for composition instruction. Pontificating on the "attitude of the average college" he writes: "The college either yearns for these persons or is timorous that a rival sister will adopt them—so it stretches out its fair arms. And obviously the next thing to do is its duty—to wean them from their illiteracy by giving them the registered milk of articulation" (9). The metaphors Thurber uses to express his views on the relationship among literacy, freshman English, and "the college" have significant implications. In *Literacy: An Introduction to the Ecology of Written Language*, David Barton touches on some of these implications when he notes:

> . . . different metaphors have different implications for how we view illiteracy, what action might be taken to change it and how we characterize the people involved. For example, if illiteracy is a disease, then the people involved are sick, it should be eradicated, and experts need to be called in to do the job. (12)

It follows that if students must be "weaned" from their illiteracy, an alternative form of sustenance must be provided. Clearly, from Thurber's perspective, instruction in what he describes as "articulation" (via belles lettres) is the preferred "treatment," but we get the sense that this approach is falling short; however, in what ways and on what levels belles lettres is deficient is not completely clear. I believe the implications of Thurber's curious use of metaphor may be made explicit by examining his quotation in the context of other metaphors used to discuss illiteracy.

In *The Social Context of Literacy*, Kenneth Levine provides a table categorizing the various ways illiteracy is sometimes characterized. David Barton provides an updated version of this table in *Literacy: An Introduction to the Ecology of Written Language.*[1]

Ways of talking about literacy (Barton 11)

Condition	Response	Means	Goal	Application
Sickness	Treatment	Clinical intervention	Remittance	
Handicap	Rehabilitation	Compensatory aids	Alleviation	Dyslexia
Ignorance	Training	Instruction	Mastery	Orthodox literacy tuition
Incapacity	Therapy	Counseling	Adjustment Assimilation Autonomy	
Oppression	Empowerment	Political organization/ Legislation	Rights	Conscientization
Deprivation	Welfare	Reallocation of material resources	Benefit	Positive discrimination
Deviance	Control	Isolation Containment Physical coercion	Correction Conformity	Negative discrimination

This table is useful because it demonstrates "how much can be achieved by looking at illiteracy through a 'wide-angle' lens and by considering the less obvious alternatives and complements to training" (Levine 172). Although it is unrealistic to expect a table like this to anticipate a "one-to-one correspondence" (172) among the conditions, responses, means, and the policies of particular institutions or the outcomes of particular systems of pedagogy, it does show multiple possibilities for considering the ways that students excluded by one mode or "condition" may find a way of "fitting in" to another category. For instance, in "Composition in Our Colleges," Thurber's reference to illiteracy is expressed through a metaphor of sustenance and consumption. In many ways, equating illiteracy with milk (and the process of weaning a child from it) cuts across Levine's categories in multiple ways and directions. By this, I mean, Thurber's figurative assessment of the issue at hand characterizes illiteracy as a "sickness," on the one hand, requiring the "registered milk of articulation" or a "treatment" via belles lettres as the response to the problem. Then again others might argue that Thurber's statement is consistent with the condition of "deprivation." That is, the "reallocation" of pedagogical materials emphasizing "articulation" may only bring about the desired "benefits" that Thurber and universities of the time seek. However, we might also understand Thurber's remarks in terms of "ignorance," in the sense that the process of "weaning students from their illiteracy" should have begun much earlier. In this way, Thurber's statement may be understood, I think, in the way he intends. To put it simply, he believes his contemporaries should be ashamed—even embarrassed—by how mismatched and inadequate prevailing approaches to literacy "training" are to the problems he identifies and by how slow they have been to react. Regardless of how Thurber's statement is understood in relation to the aforementioned conditions, treatments, and goals, his statement demonstrates that he is doubtful of composition's ability to provide the type of instruction and training necessary to mitigate what he perceives to be an illiteracy crisis. The solution that Thurber proposes, which I turn to now, demonstrates a desire to reorient writing instruction away from solving illiteracy in students and toward facilitating the trend toward academic specialization. Unlike Lounsbury, Thurber does not seem opposed to the consequences of specialization. In fact, the alternative model for writing instruction that he proposes depends in large part on the segmentation and further development of disciplines. What becomes clear in Thurber's statement, in a way that Lounsbury does not reveal, is the extent to which he envisions writing instruction as functioning to undergird academic specialization in universities more generally.

This aspect of his argument becomes clear when we examine how Thurber feels about composition textbooks, belles lettres, and the repetitive nature of prevailing pedagogical approaches to composition. After deriding freshman English textbooks for being more appropriate for English instructors than students (10), Thurber proceeds to a critique of rhetoric itself. He notes: "In our modern college, the teaching of expression appears to be given over almost entirely to a synod of aesthetes. To them, for instance, Plato is not so much a figure in philosophy as a figure of expression" (11). For Thurber, emphasis on the modes of discourse is unnecessary and ultimately gives way to assignments comprised of repetitive drills.[2] "Yesterday the class studied about a steam engine," he asserts, "today it takes up the history of a piece of chalk; tomorrow it is to examine how well a man gives the impression of the height of a cathedral, or it may note the choice phraseology of a lyric" (11). Although Thurber's antagonism toward rhetoric, belles lettres, and the repetitive nature of writing pedagogy in the early 1900s is commonplace (and as I noted in my introduction, we find similar frustrations and complaints levied against rhetorical instruction today), Thurber's proposed solution is distinct in at least one way, and it sets him apart from his contemporaries. That is, his essay may be understood as one of the earliest arguments for abolishing composition in favor of an arrangement that divides the responsibility of writing instruction among the various disciplines that constitute universities.

"By my side," Thurber writes, "is a book entitled *Handbook of English for Engineers*. It is compiled by a 'professor' of English and with it goes a book of "specimens" emanating from a department of English" (12).[3] Thurber seems vexed by the fact that the authors (or "compilers") of the text consider the essay more appropriate for "Upper classmen" (12). This announcement prompts a series of rhetorical questions touching on multiple topics, among them the extent to which high schools fail to prepare students for college. That said, this is not his principal complaint. His chief concern grows out of an interest in whether freshman English courses are relevant to students' interests. Thurber poses succinctly his central problem with composition:

> In many of our colleges, however, perhaps in the majority of them, the very fact that the average teacher of composition is concerned primarily with imaginative literature, belles lettres, provokes an endless search for subjects quite other than those in which the students are supposed to be engrossed. And to this delusion is responsible in large measure, I take it, the bankruptcy of the freshman course. (13)

His solution is to impose a "fixed doctrine" so that each group of students would "be guided in its writing by an expert" (14). For Thurber, agriculture students should be taught composition by "one who is vitally interested"

(14) in agriculture. Likewise, engineers "should be taught composition by instructors interested in subjects that engineers are interested in" (14). A few months after "Composition in Our Colleges" appears in *The English Journal*, we find Thurber stating his position even more directly in his letter to the editor in the September 1915 issue of *The Nation*, asking "Why have the departments of English in our colleges been carrying the entire burden of composition?" Thurber's statements reveal his frustration with how English departments have come to be solely responsible for "weaning" students from their illiteracy. And in *The Nation*, he provides a sobering assessment of what will likely follow if expectations of freshman English are not reevaluated in relation to the needs of students and universities. He writes: "The department of English is straining to become a forum of discussion of all questions that have assailed human intelligence" (328). If rectifying the ostensible problem of illiteracy is to continue to be the aim of freshman English, then Thurber desires a pedagogical configuration across specialties in universities that will allow "mature minds" and instruction in articulation and "expression" to keep "pace with concern in subject-matter" (14).

In sum, Thurber's position may be stated quite simply: The problem of illiteracy is not solved with freshman composition, articulation, or instruction in rhetoric or poetics. The course is unable to do its job for two reasons. First and foremost, the thematic focus of freshman English is not relevant to students' needs. From Thurber's perspective, prevailing approaches to writing instruction are repetitive and based on antiquated principles of rhetoric. His solution is to reposition the responsibility of writing instruction in universities so that students work with experts in particular disciplines to learn to write for particular fields and specialties. Second, the course aspires to solve a problem that seems to defy solution; namely, illiteracy. Because freshman English has taken on the task of solving the problem of illiteracy, Thurber believes it has become a site for "discussion of all questions that have assailed human intelligence" (328). Thurber's "Composition in Our Colleges" demonstrates how attempting to solve the problem of illiteracy via composition throws into relief the limits of compulsory writing instruction. As is the case during Thurber's time, making these limits visible also meant making the course less relevant to the emerging needs of universities in the early 1900s.

The following study, by Frederick A. Manchester, demonstrates a similar preoccupation with questioning the exaggerated expectations that surround the aims of compulsory composition. However, as we will see, Manchester questions both the extent to which freshman English may solve the perceived problem of illiteracy, and whether compulsory composition should be responsible for the "moral welfare" of its students.

WITH CURIOSITY AND COMPASSION— FRESHMAN ENGLISH ONCE MORE

Writing from the University of Wisconsin–Madison in 1917, Frederick Manchester begins his study with a bold statement: "The problem of Freshman English as it confronts us in our large middle-western universities is incapable of a satisfying solution" (295).[4] After remarking sarcastically on the "ridiculously" short amount of time for instruction and the "abundance of wisely selected" readings and texts that comprise the pedagogical apparatus of the course, Manchester proceeds to a series of recommendations that are as interesting for their scope as they are for their contradictions. Published six years after Lounsbury's "Compulsory College Composition" and four years after Thurber's "Composition in Our Colleges," Manchester proposes a series of goals for the course which suggest significant continuities in the Great Debate over compulsory composition. As I will argue below, these continuities reveal the varied ways that myths of literacy underline the Great Debate during this period. When this is the case, the distinction between abolitionists and reformists (one put forth by Connors and Russell) becomes more difficult to maintain.

Manchester's first proposal for reform is related to the overall "function" of freshman English. For him, freshman English "can afford" to have one aim, and one aim only: "the cultivation in the student of a mastery of self-expression in English speech" (298), an outcome achieved by resisting the tendency to generalize the function of the course to other aims and ends. He writes:

> It means that we shall not consider ourselves responsible for the moral welfare of our students, nor for their orientation in college life, nor for their education in citizenship, nor for their enlightenment with respect to the general conceptions of biology, political economy, history, or religion; it means that we shall steadily refuse to be distracted from our particular task by any irrelevant aim whatsoever. (298)

And so, for Manchester, it is by "simplifying the function," or resisting a penchant for what he describes as "instruction in ideas" (299) that freshman English may come to do its intended duty and achieve its second goal.

The second goal that Manchester proposes is related "at bottom to a question of emphasis" (299). "One of the most baneful of education doctrines," he writes, "is the doctrine that it is better to teach what is relatively unimportant and be sure of success than to teach what is truly essential and run the risk of failure" (299–300). This inclination, according to Manchester, is one to which instructors are "naturally disposed" because the task of teaching "mastery of expression" is so difficult and complex that aspects of instruction that are more easily teachable tend to occupy their time. For instance, he seems perplexed by the time spent examining "logical structure" and the attention spent on "analyzing essays which exhibit complex trains of thought" (300). With respect to grammar, Manchester sees an "acquaintance with grammar" as "indispensable" (300), and he acknowledges that "it is a pity that our students when they come to us are not better grounded in the subject" (300), but he notes instructors of freshman English "cannot afford" to focus on grammar at the expense of instruction in and mastery of expression in the mother-tongue (301). Furthermore, Manchester is unconvinced by preoccupations with both grammar and philology, which he notes belong more to the study of language "as an abstract science than to language as an instrument of expression" (301). To put it simply, Manchester's ideal curriculum in freshman English *seems* to be constituted by the history, theory, and lesson of rhetoric, but this is an idea he will qualify extensively in the second part of his study.

Emphasis in rhetoric specifically is Manchester's third suggestion, and it is one that reflects previously noted academic pressures and reforms of the time. He emphasizes the importance of providing what he describes as "an intellectual challenge" to students of both biology and chemistry, asserting "I see no reason why a young man who can be made to understand the formidable abstractions of other subjects should not be expected to assimilate equally difficult conceptions in the art of rhetoric" (302). For Manchester, freshman English should provide students the intellectual challenge of mastery in the art of rhetoric, and it should do so because rhetoric provides a means of preserving the "true spirit" of a university (302). However, in 1917—when Manchester publishes his study—the "true spirit" and aims of the university are being pulled in multiple directions by proponents of academic specialization on the one hand, and the generalist opposition on the other.

According to Gerald Graff, the generalist opposition defined itself against "specialized investigators" (81), or those in favor of further segmenting universities along disciplinary lines. They emphasized humanism in the development of English studies with the hope of "adapting the old college ideal of liberal culture to the challenges of modern times" (85). Like Thurber's, Manchester's argument in "Freshman English Once More" seems both opposed to and sympathetic to further specialization. On the one hand, he argues for renewed focus on "our task, and swinging back to the center, re-establishing there and not elsewhere a substantial discipline" (304). Yet, he cautions against the tendency of universities "which is by nature selective" and "embraces all the world" (303). He argues for a narrowing of the scope of freshman English to the study of rhetoric, yet he explicitly states "we can surely agree that Freshman English must resist the temptation to minister to all the needs of man, in order that it may concentrate on its particular task; that it must steadily oppose the natural tendency to substitute the simple parts of this task for the whole" (305). Sounding very much like Thurber when he laments that English departments have become a site for "discussion of all questions that have assailed human intelligence" (Thurber 328), Manchester questions the idea that freshman English should be responsible solely for the moral welfare and citizenship of students. In spite of this, however, the course provides an opportunity to fulfill "a special responsibility," for "every activity," he writes, has its "specific good" (299), specifically "the preservation in its methods of the true spirit of a university" (302). From this perspective, it is easy to see why Manchester characterizes freshman English as "a makeshift" and "temporary device," a "mere Sphinx riddle defying solution" (296). Freshman English, in Manchester's eyes, is simply trying to do too much.

To a great extent, we may understand Manchester as caught in between the two camps of "specialized investigators" and "the generalist opposition." Gerald Graff notes that by 1915, two years before Manchester's article was published, "a curious mixture of overconfidence and defeatism" defines scholarship in English studies. "Reformers," he writes, "whose vision goes no further than making their subject hard" become increasingly susceptible to criticisms of superficiality or simply being labeled as "not knowing what to do with" their proposed reforms. Clearly, Manchester is feeling these pressures specifically. After all, he anticipates such objections when remarking on reforming freshman English toward the vaguely defined aim of preserving "true spirit of a university," specifically noting, "I now insist that superficiality or insignificance is farthest from my thoughts" (301). Manchester's somewhat contradictory proposals for reform point to the ways in which "the gulf between" specialized investigators and generalists "was never absolute" (G. Graff 81), but Manchester's ambivalence reflects something of more importance, at least with respect to the abolition debate. More than anything else, Manchester's essay reveals the influence of confiding in the literacy myth.

"FRESHMAN ENGLISH ONCE MORE—CONCLUDED"

The impact of overstating the importance of literacy is evident in the way Manchester's essay transforms from an argument indebted to abolitionist rhetoric in part one, to one that reads more like a reformist argument in part two. This shift in tone is significant because it parallels another development in Manchester's attitude toward literacy. In contrast to the broad scope of part one, which was published only one month before the second part in June, 1917, "Freshman English Once More—Concluded" is devoted solely to Manchester's fourth and final recommendation: reforming freshman English with an emphasis on reading. Unlike the first part of his study, which begins and ends with a decidedly cynical characterization of what he describes as the "insoluble" problem of freshman English, the second half is generally optimistic and pragmatic. Nevertheless, I will show that like other voices in the Great Debate, Manchester's study relies on a rhetoric of crisis that stems specifically from myths of literacy. What makes his proposal distinct from other reformist essays is the way his exaggerated expectations about the consequences of being literate are connected to his tendency to overstate the significance of reading practices. Furthermore, and as I mentioned, Manchester's attitudes about literacy parallel a distinctive shift in tone, which I take up now.

Manchester's shift in tone is important to note because it exemplifies his ambivalence about freshman English, which is linked to his general frustrations with composition outlined in the first part of his article. When he remarks on the "adverse conditions" of freshman English he asserts, "It is surely no wonder that in large measure we fail; the wonder is, when one thinks of it, that we succeed at all" (295). However, in the conclusion of his second part he finishes on a more affirmative note:

> Freshman English, it is true, is not a very impressive thing in the economy of the world or of the university, but if we study its possibilities on an ideal plane and remember how many thousands and thousands of students come yearly within the scope of its influence, we shall not fail to realize that it has an important claim upon our serious consideration. (398)

Just as important as explicating why Manchester believes that freshman English is not "a very impressive thing" in the world or university, or how the expression "ideal plane" functions in this passage, is explaining how and why his message transforms so dramatically between its two parts. A key part of understanding this transformation can be found in the unspoken assumption that bolsters his entire study. "We can count on a general conviction," he writes, "among influential men in all walks of life that the ability to use English well is important; and what people consider important they will provide for" (398). Curiously, differences between what Manchester desires and what "influential men in all walks of life" want become apparent when we examine the role that reading plays in his proposed curriculum for freshman English.

According to Manchester, freshman English students may be taught how to "use English well" by employing a pedagogy that is "intensive" in "central reading" and "extensive" with respect to "general reading" (384). Intensive reading of Greek or Latin writers is to be prescribed in "limited amounts" in order to provide students with what the "earlier generation obtained from their minute study of the classics," specifically, the acquisition of taste and style as well as "an intimate understanding of what is really involved in accurate and masterly expression" (385). For Manchester, this understanding is not achieved by prevailing methods of pedagogy of his time. "It will not come to them," he writes, "from an occasional use of the dictionary, nor from listening to general discourse on the subject-matter of their reading, nor even, I fear, from the endless production of logical outlines." To be sure, as the first part of his essay makes clear, Manchester is categorically opposed to the repetitive drills that comprise writing textbooks and instruction of his day. But his fixation on the "ancient classics" is also a response to educational reforms that have made these works less relevant. He writes:

> There can be little doubt that the ancient classics, especially in this country, have suffered greatly from the absence in many of their representatives of a truly humanistic spirit. The study which should have challenged every faculty, whether of observation or reflection, has only too often been restricted to the narrow dimensions of a linguistic science. (385)

Manchester is speaking, in part, to the effects of the rise of philology, an approach to language and pedagogy in English studies that is linked to English departments' struggle to gain a respected place in the university. Although Manchester questions the consequences of English's fixation on science, he recognizes its importance in graduate student education, which is directly connected to his plan for reforming freshman English. "In fixing attention upon the importance of exact knowledge," he writes, "and in making a mastery of external fact an essential preliminary to criticism, the scientific work of our graduate schools has, no doubt, been of real service, not merely to the future investigator, but likewise to the future interpreter of literature" (396). In other words, Manchester seems to recognize the value of philology as a legitimizing force in the development of English departments, but the essence of his argument is that the "faithful and intimate study of what is excellent" (389) trumps commitments to science. For Manchester, "facts" are but a foundation for a "mission" in "another and far more difficult region" (396). Further complicating intensive reading in freshman English is the "cult of the contemporary," a movement which he notes "appears to be spreading throughout our schools" at an "alarming rate" (390). Manchester rejects specifically the notion that "what is produced in the present has for the student a strength of appeal that does not attach to the writings of an earlier period" (389). He contends that the cult of the contemporary is motivated by "superficial" and "utterly false" notions of both students and the classics. He extends his criticism to instructors as well, noting that if students are not interested in intensive study of the classics "it is because they have not understood them; and whatever unusual obstacles appear as a hindrance to understanding it, it is the business of the teacher to remove" (390). For Manchester the classics—including the English classics of the nineteenth century—are remote, and it is only through the practice of "intensiveness" that students may experience "a profound satisfaction in the presence of a richness of thought" (390). I emphasize this aspect of his proposal here because I believe the language he uses betrays a particular attitude toward literacy. Manchester's notion of "intensive" reading presumes inherent qualities—"richness of thought" and "masterly expression"—of both the act of reading and the written word (Street 44). Certainly, Manchester's view is consistent with the ways that "strong" theories of literacy overstate the significance of possessing it. Even more important to note, however, is how his understanding of literacy leads him to an overly simplistic characterization of the pedagogical processes that he believes should constitute composition instruction.

Related to the first principle of "intensiveness" is Manchester's second suggestion for a curriculum in reading. Somewhat predictably, he refers to this approach as "extensiveness," and without it "intensiveness" alone is an insufficient means of realizing his aims for freshman English (390). Even worse, employing one without the other, may lead to "stiffness and formalism" in student writing (391). It is only by utilizing both reading practices simultaneously that the "natural background for the practice of composition" is established. In contrast to intensive reading, which is intended to teach students "what enlightened reading is," extensive reading is concerned with what Manchester describes as "general reading." The assumption supporting this notion is that by exposing students to "varying words and phrases and sentences," students will attain "freedom of expression" (391). However, one curious aspect of this notion is that how extensive reading is employed is not as important as ensuring that it happens. Manchester states specifically, "It matters little what system is employed to secure general reading" (391). This is because, according to Manchester, the "first-year curriculum" is so "crowded" that it is unrealistic to expect a student to "read any very great amount during the time we have charge of him" (391). Despite this, Manchester maintains that students must, at least, attempt "general reading." Without it, "intensive" reading becomes futile, as the "natural background" of freshman English falls away (391).

Manchester's description of extensive reading is remarkable in that it belies so much of what he outlines in his discussion of intensive reading.

Intensive reading is supposedly *limited* to what he identifies as the classics; quantity is not important. In fact, on this point he states specifically: "We shall never remotely approximate the ideal until we are ready to limit the amount of reading which we do to a degree which will at first appear extraordinary, until we perceive that what really matters is not *how much* we read but *how* we read" (387). Yet, Manchester never really discusses "how" to read (instead he repeatedly prescribes *what* to read), and the specifics of his discussion of extensive reading are limited to issues of quantity. After all, he calls it *extensive* reading, an expression used to emphasize a sum total of reading necessary to realize the goals of his curriculum. For Manchester, the principles of expression are achieved by the "maximum amount" of general reading (390), and it is "only through wide reading, through endlessly repeated contact" with varying words and phrases that the benefits of extensive reading may be experienced by students. Furthermore, the contradictions of his proposal, especially those contradictions tied to notions of quantity, are exemplified in his final recommendation when he suggests that the "insoluble" problem of freshman English may be solved—somewhat unbelievably—by requiring *more* writing. He writes: "Let us require training in English, not for one year only, but in one form or another for two years or even three years" (397). Like so many proposals for abolition or reform (in the case of Manchester he performs both moves) "Freshman English Once More" is a study in contradictions, and there is a sense in which Manchester is caught in the contradictions that constitute his own understanding of the powers of reading and writing. In this way, the contradictions that emerge from Manchester's essay, with respect to his shifting tone and inconsistent recommendations, may be linked to his attitude about literacy, specifically his abiding belief in allowing reading and writing alone to develop the faculties of taste and judgment.

Harvey J. Graff writes that "To understand literacy means that contradictions should be expected to result from the ongoing processes and developments within culture, polity, economy, and society. These are neither ironic nor paradoxical, as some call them, but fundamentally *historical*" (*The Legacies of Literacy* 10). As I will demonstrate, the inherent contradictions in Manchester's argument have broader implications for the study of the abolition debate on two levels: First, they reveal the ways that literacy functions as both a learning outcome for freshman English and a participant in the construction of that outcome. Second, they reveal how the promoted value of literacy contradicts the more restricted function of literacy in freshman English.

In *Literacy in Theory and Practice*, Brian V. Street challenges what he describes as the autonomous conceptions of literacy, a model that defines and presents literacy as separate from the social contexts that give it meaning. In demonstrating that the autonomous model is based on ethnocentric notions of reading and writing practices, Street connects the autonomous model to the Western academic tradition specifically. For instance, in academic contexts he describes how the "distance between addresser and addressee is theoretically at a maximum, and communication is at its most impersonal" (75). According to Street, this distance between academic texts and students serves to justify one aim of the autonomous model: to understand writing and reading practices as neutral or objective. In the classroom, this model translates into a curriculum that organizes learning in a way where students are asked to make sense of 'the words on the page'" (75). "Students are taught," he writes, "to 'read' in a different way from that of everyday practice: rather than reading a text from beginning to end in the sequence in which the publisher has ordered it" (75). Taken together, this conception of literacy and its pedagogical application may be understood to constitute "academic language" (75). It is one, he notes, that is burdened by "significant claims," and these claims "derive from the requirements which brought it into being in the first place" (76). The implications of Street's assertions for the abolition debate are clear in the ways that Manchester's essay relies on a distinction between oral and literate discourse.

While the second part of "Freshman English Once More" is preoccupied with reading practices, the first part is concerned primarily with what Manchester describes as "articulation" and "masterful expression" of the English language. Although the amount of space Manchester allots to both sections seems evenhanded, the powers and claims he ascribes to the practices of intensive and extensive reading are far more strongly emphasized. One key characteristic of a strong theory of literacy, which depends on a characterization of literacy based on the autonomous model, is the tendency to conflate speech with writing, a tendency we see in the first section of Manchester's study, where he proclaims boldly, "I am ready to maintain that Freshman English can afford to have one object and one only: The cultivation in the student of a mastery of self-expression in English speech" (298). From this perspective, the oral aspects of rhetoric become the primary emphasis of freshman English. However, when Manchester concludes his essay and presents his strategy for persuading university "officers" to adopt what sounds like a modern-day vertical curriculum for freshman English (in which students are required to take writing courses over an extended period of time) the relationship between his prescribed reading practices and writing become more important. He notes:

> Once the English teachers of this country are agreed that the writing of our students will never be what it ought to be until more time is spent in the reading of literature and in the practice of composition, and once they present their unanimous conclusion to the university officers, I believe they will be heard. We can count

> on a general conviction among influential men in all walks of life that the ability to use English well is important; and what people consider important they will provide for. (398)

The various versions that literacy takes (as speech, writing, and reading) as well as the characteristics and powers that Manchester ascribes to each of them, anticipate Street's notion of the autonomous model. Manchester's insistence that articulation and expression must be considered separately from reading and writing depends, in part, on the assumption that the primary function of writing is to represent speech. It also presumes that writing does not perform functions or possess characteristics independent of speech (Street 66). Magnifying this confusion even further is that the type of well-spoken English to which Manchester refers in the above passage is associated with more common usages of vernacular English, not essayist literacy or composition in the academic tradition. Furthermore, how Manchester uses the expressions "articulation" and "English speech" also suggests, to some degree, that he is simultaneously conflating *and* distinguishing between speech and writing. In Manchester's study, we find that the promoted value of literacy in his curriculum is consistent with the perceived needs of the university (as articulated by university "officers"), but when we consider his specific suggestions for how to instruct students in speech, writing, and reading in freshman English itself, we find a discrepancy between what universities need and what composition is able to provide. Despite how mismatched Manchester's solutions are to a problem that he readily admits defies solution, "Freshman English Once More" relies on a rhetoric of crisis that depends on myths of literacy as well as the ambiguous and inconsistent definitions of literacy that make those myths possible. Ultimately, instead of affecting change on any meaningful level, Manchester's study actually perpetuates the problems that he seeks to address.

But perhaps the most striking lesson to be learned from Manchester's study is that his statements about literacy and composition in 1917 were harbingers of things to come. In 1948, we find Manchester contributing a chapter to the fifth edition of *Composition for College Students: A guide for the study and effective writing of good English, with abundant illustrative examples from many authors.*[5] Titled "On the Use of the Library and Related Topics," the chapter is divided into five sections. The fourth part, "On Writing Examinations," concerns itself with what Manchester describes as five types of "Demons": The Demon of Irrelevancy, The Demon of Diffuseness, The Demon of Generality, The Demon of Disorderliness, and lamentably, the Demon of Illiteracy. According to Manchester, the demon of irrelevancy is deserving of "a place at the head of list" (643). It corresponds with the "setting down of matter which has nothing to do with the question." Diffuseness, on the other hand, describes writing that provides an "ocean of words" but a "thimbleful of thought" (643). And as one might expect, the demons of Generality and Disorderliness are responsible for overly general and unstructured prose. It is the demon of Illiteracy, however, that causes "bad spelling, bad punctuation, wrong use or nonuse of apostrophe, bad grammar and generally incorrect sentence structure" (646). In most other contexts, it would make sense, I think, to connect Manchester's rhetoric to religious and spiritual underpinnings. After all, characterizing perceived inadequacies in student writing as demons to be conjured, controlled, resisted—even exorcised—raises compelling questions about the impact of Manchester's religious background on his attitudes about freshman English.[6] Nevertheless, I mention this small excerpt from Manchester's co-authored textbook because I wish to highlight the trajectory of Manchester's thinking about literacy over time.

Published 31 years after his critique of composition, Manchester's 1948 argument for the importance of reading (and its influence on writing and thinking) remains awash in metaphor and complicated by ambiguous definitions. And as alarming as his rhetoric may be, his taxonomy of demonic devices actually represents a conventional and rather persistent approach to understanding literacy, especially in contemporary higher education. At bottom, Manchester's list of demons is principally concerned with breaking down literacy into smaller parts, as each of his demons corresponds with a particular set of skills or subskills. To be sure, in this case, Manchester's formulation of reading and writing skills represents an inverse correlation, as the demons of "Irrelevancy," "Diffuseness," "Generality," "Disorderliness," and "Illiteracy" are to be avoided. However, accompanying each demon is a recommendation from Manchester emphasizing a particular practice or series of subskills intended to "drive out" the evil spirit. The demon of Illiteracy, for instance, manifests itself when students are unprepared or lazy. "The best proof of genuine literacy," Manchester asserts, "is the ability to preserve it under stress . . . The best preparation, it need hardly be said, is steady work throughout the semester, not hectic study near its end" (646). The type of work Manchester has in mind follows an orderly plan that begins with "arming yourself with a first-rate dictionary," (648) proceeds to learning how to deduce meaning in sentences first, then paragraphs, and finally, chapters. At stake for Manchester is the development of intellectual aptitude in students. He writes: "Every successful effort of the kind which you make represents definite progress in the cultivation of your mental powers" (649). Presumably, every effort students make also brings them closer to freeing themselves from the demon that supposedly afflicts them.

In *Literacy: An Introduction to the Ecology of Written Language*, David Barton reminds us that the "idea of skills is a particular way of thinking about literacy; it is a metaphor no less than the disease metaphor" (12). As such, the significance of Manchester's list of reading and writing skills has little to do with the fact that he draws from religious terminology to enhance the persuasive appeal of his chapter, "On The Use of The Library." Rather, what is so striking about Manchester's list of demons is that they represent a way of talking about and understanding literacy as an independent variable and set of skills. One implication of deconstructing literacy into a set of skills, according to Barton, is that literacy is sometimes seen only "as a psychological variable which can be measured and assessed." "Skills are treated as things," Barton writes, "which people own or possess; some are *transferable* skills, some are not" (12). My argument is that Manchester's own demons are the net result of an uncritical way of thinking about literacy and illiteracy over an extended period of time. We see evidence of this in Manchester's tendency to characterize "genuine literacy" as a sort of state of grace, only attainable by those students who have defeated their demons and gained particular skills through hard work, which as Manchester points out, "is the secret, as in most often accomplishments" (648). Just as with the "disease," "handicap," and "deviance" metaphors, how we talk about and view literacy always determines the actions we take to influence it as well as how we characterize the people involved (Barton 12). When we compare Manchester's 1917 critique of composition with his 1948 textbook chapter, we find a trajectory of thinking that characterizes literacy as a skill-based, technical dilemma with the only solution being found in hard work. This view makes possible Manchester's graphic representations of literacy and illiteracy as demonic spirits; however, more significantly, Manchester's view also characterizes freshman English students as either lazy—for not demonstrating genuine literacy under pressure—or possessed by evil spirits because of inadequate mental powers. It is safe to say that Manchester's students found themselves in a difficult position both in 1917 and in 1948.

Much like Thurber's essay, Manchester's argument is chiefly concerned with spreading out the burden of composition instruction across the university. In the first part of his 1917 essay, as I discussed, he advocates an approach to writing instruction that aspired to mitigate the consequences of academic specialization. However, because the "burden" or "problems" of composition in these studies are inextricably linked to inconsistent definitions of literacy as well as the tendency to confide in literacy myths, both Thurber and Manchester reveal how the rhetoric of abolitionism is rooted in and responding not just to institutional pressures but also to exaggerated expectations for freshman English, expectations that are inextricably linked with latent attitudes about literacy. On the surface, both Thurber's and

Manchester's arguments to abolish composition appear to address the many weaknesses that the two authors marshal as evidence of the ineffectiveness of composition. In the end, though, both authors' proposed solutions are merely temporary stopgaps for their own unrealistic expectations and uncritical ways of talking about and understanding literacy. With this point in mind, and when considered in the context of Manchester's essay specifically, it becomes possible to understand how the rhetoric of abolitionism offers no solutions to the problem of freshman English. Instead, it circulates the myths and characterizations of literacy that situate it as an independent variable, understandings of literacy that perpetuate the cycle of abolitionism itself.

As we find in the following critique of composition, one way of dealing with these exaggerated expectations, and the inevitable disappointment that accompanies them, is to place the blame and burden of solving the perceived problem of teaching composition on to secondary schools. Although this is an issue I discuss more fully in the following chapter, I introduce it now because it underscores yet another continuity in the debate over compulsory composition. As I have shown, evaluating the relationship of literacy to proposals for the abolition of composition requires an expanded view of the debate, one that resists the tendency to characterize participants as "new" or "old," but instead searches for similarities and continuities. In the following study by Paulinus Lange, ambiguous understandings of literacy as well as the tendency to overstate its significance are the most perceptible continuities. However, the implications of these attitudes about literacy are different from previously discussed essays in this chapter. This is because in Lange's essay, myths of literacy and exaggerated expectations of the consequences of possessing it underline a proposal that professes an abiding belief in the ability of achievement tests to solve the problem of compulsory composition in post-secondary and secondary education.

WHAT PRICE ENGLISH? THE COSTS OF GENERALIZING THE LITERACY MYTH TO THE UNIVERSITY

It is interesting that almost forty years pass in the history of the abolition debate with respect to studies that recommend that high schools rather than universities should become the site of composition instruction. Although Leonard Greenbaum notes that arguments for greater attention to composition at the high school and preparatory levels are a part of a "tradition of complaint," his history does not discuss the issue at length. Likewise, Connors and Russell only make glancing references to abolitionists that take up the issue of high schools. For instance, in his study, "The New Abolitionism," Connors points to B. S. Hurlbut's "College Requirements in English" as an example of a study seeking to replace freshman English with more effective composition instruction at the high school level. Published in 1896, Hurlbut argues that "[t]he instruction in English which we are forced to give to Freshmen and perhaps to Sophomores should all be finished in the preparatory schools" (Connors 5). Hurlbut felt it "absurd" that colleges should have to take on the task of teaching spelling, pronunciation, and grammar. From his perspective, only reforms at the elementary and secondary levels would provide students the training necessary to allow students to devote their time to "university work" (5).

According to Russell and Greenbaum, however, the most notable reference to relegating instruction in composition to high schools comes from Warner G. Rice's NCTE convention address in 1959. Eventually published in *College English* in 1960, and titled "A Proposal for the Abolition of Freshman English, As It Is Now Commonly Taught, from the College Curriculum," Rice's position is quite clear; composition should *only* be taught at the high school level, and once removed from the college curriculum, absolutely nothing should replace it. Greenbaum notes that Rice was familiar with the workings of college administration, and this knowledge might have allowed him to anticipate and swiftly refute objections about the changes needed to finance graduate education or other reforms after abolishing freshman English. Yet although Rice's argument is the most well-known in histories of writing instruction, he was preceded by similar arguments over twenty years earlier.

As mentioned in the previous chapter, Robert Connors remarks on the decade of the 1930s as a period of "lively discussion of reform and abolition," more lively than had ever occurred before with respect to proposals to abolish or reform freshman English. He also points out that the nature and tenor of these debates was "incredibly contemporary." The field saw debates dealing with "proposals for English as training for social experience, for Marxist critique in the classroom, for writing across the curriculum, for research-based reforms of various kinds, for more or less literary influence on composition, and for better conditions for teachers" (13). Consequently, during the 1930s, composition found itself in a difficult spot. In one sense, it was mired in debates over its effectiveness and value in the college curriculum, yet as John Guillory notes in *Cultural Capital,* it was also taking on a "new institutional significance," performing what he describes as "a new social function for the university, the task of providing the future technobureaucractic elite with precisely and only the linguistic competence necessary for the performance of its specialized functions" (264). Another plausible explanation for composition's enhanced relevance during this time is that the late 1930s are also a period marked by the economic dislocations of the Great Depression as well as the beginning of WWII. These events, as many histories of English attest, led to increased enrollments in universities, making composition an essential part of the project of keeping up with the demand of increasing enrollments. For instance, in *On a Scale: A Social History of Writing Assessment in America*, Norbert Elliot confirms these increased enrollments and notes, "college enrollment had risen nearly 50 percent between 1899–1900 and 1909–1910. In the following decade, enrollment rose by 68 percent. Between 1919–1920 and 1929–1930, enrollment rose by 84 percent" (85).

It is in this lively period of increasing enrollments and pressures that Paulus Lange publishes "What Price English?" Like Thurber's study and Manchester's textbook chapter, Lange's article is not discussed at length by existing histories of the great debate. Interestingly, Lange's study is also inconsistent with Connors' findings and challenges, to some degree, Guillory's claims about composition gaining "a new institutional significance." Writing in 1938, Lange is concerned with improving the conditions of learning for both teachers and students of English composition, but he is also apprehensive about the rising costs of things in the university, specifically freshman composition. In "What Price English?" he states his position emphatically:

> The ultimate elimination of freshman composition will give the English Department an opportunity to devote itself to its proper function, namely, that of offering courses not only in language, literature, and related fields but also in advanced composition to those students who desire to develop the more mature qualities of style which are beyond even the best high-school achievement. (427)

Similar to other proposals for abolition I have examined, Lange is motivated by the "more mature qualities of style," yet he is also responding to a sense of crisis. "Society has grown more and more complex," he writes, "and the problems arising out of that condition have become distressingly acute" (424). He does not explicate these problems precisely, except to note, like many critics of composition before him, that the departmentalization of "subject-matter" has had "pernicious effects" on the teaching of spoken and written English (424). Lange's quotation indicates that he is responding, in part, to the consequences of academic specialization. However, more significant is the vague sense of crisis underlining Lange's argument. Certainly, as many would argue, Lange's claims about the "problems arising" out of an increasingly complex society are intended to create a sense of urgency for his audience. This may be true, but as Harvey J. Graff and others remind us, appeals to crisis intended to "heighten the sensitivity" (*The Labyrinths of Literacy* 321) of proposed educational reforms have their costs. In Lange's case, it turns out that the cost is quite high; in fact, I believe that his study is one of the most instructive examples of how criticisms of composition relying on appeals to crisis and decline actually serve to perpetuate the very problems they seek to resolve.

Simply put, notions of crisis in "What Price English?"—as well as Lange's persistent belief that composition is in perpetual decline—restrict the scope of his understanding of the problems at hand. One consequence is that the solutions he proposes also narrow in step. For instance, Lange laments the "departmentalization of subject matter" (424)—or the trend toward academic specialization—for creating the institutional conditions that lead to poor writing of students. Yet he places most of the blame for the "pernicious" effects he perceives in student writing with ineffective instruction at the high school level. "Not only do we get from the high schools," he writes, "what we are willing to accept, but subsequently we put our own stamp of approval on our own negligence" (428). If students are unable to demonstrate particular literacy practices upon application to universities, Lange does not want them admitted. I emphasize this last point because when we consider passages like these in the context of the solutions Lange proposes (which I touch on in the next section), we find that his essay is an early example of how high schools become the lone scapegoat for the problems of freshman English.

Much like Thurber's and Manchester's studies, Lange's essay is invested in maintaining literacy myths, and it also relies on ambiguous statements about what counts as being literate. However, unlike his predecessors, whose vague definitions of literacy led them to believe that the problems of freshman English could be resolved through more effective instruction and training, Lange's understanding of the problem at hand and the solutions he proposes are inextricably linked with and restricted by the appeals to crisis that foreground his argument. Harvey J. Graff's scholarship on appeals to "crisis" and "decline" in the history of literacy sheds light on what is at stake in my examination of Lange. Graff writes: "Quantity and quality are confused; educational purpose is distorted. The consequent fears of 'crisis' and 'decline' rigidly narrow the frame of education—including literacy itself—and all but guarantee the repetition of the cycle" (*The Labyrinths of Literacy* 331). Unlike Thurber and Manchester, who seek to deal internally (within the university and at the departmental level) with the consequences of confiding in the literacy myth, Lange believes that the problem of freshman English belongs to someone besides English departments, namely, high school English teachers. Furthermore, his myopic view of the problem, as I have noted, grows out of a poorly defined and vague sense of crisis that Lange suggests surrounds freshman English. It is this narrowing of "the frame of education" (Graff 331) that leads Lange to an even more limited solution: admission tests. In Lange's view, the only way for English departments to avoid putting a "stamp of approval" on their own "negligence" is to implement an achievement test that will act as a "prerequisite to unqualified admission" (425).

The achievement test that Lange has in mind, he remarks, is "necessary" and "by no means untried" (425). He points specifically to Brown University as an example of an institution that has adopted his plan. Of this test, "The Reporter" section of the *Journal of Higher Education* (1937) wrote:

> The requirements for the B.A. degree have been changed by Brown University this fall. Proficiency tests will be used so that students who show sufficient ability in English composition and in a reading knowledge of a foreign language will not be required to take these subjects. (445)

Brown was certainly not the only university experimenting with achievement tests in the late 1930s. In fact, on June 21, 1937, one year before the publication of Lange's essay, 7,000 college applicants "from Maine to California in the United States, and in such foreign cities as London, Paris, Berlin, Geneva, and Shanghai" sat down to complete a 190-minute writing examination (Noyes and Stalnaker qtd. in Elliot 108). The test these candidates completed was based on a new system developed by William Merritt Sale, Jr., of Cornell University and H. E. Joyce of Dartmouth. At stake in the new approach was the issue of how to assess essay examinations in a way that would increase reader-reliability and consistency of results of essay examinations, but would not be divisive to scholars in the humanities and the sciences.

Writing in the *English Journal* in 1936, John Stalnaker, a professor of psychology at Princeton University, remarks on the "antagonistic feelings" between those in the sciences and humanities about the test construction (qtd. in Elliot 103). And although he believes that an "English examination which is sound from every point of view" (133) is possible, he critiques current methods (specifically, the College Board's English essay examination) for lacking reliability. Part of the problem, was the "psychology" of the readers (103), which was made worse by the fact that the topics available in the 1936 examination were thematically flawed. For instance, "wise" students would choose topics like "[s]omething in contemporary music, sculpture, painting, or architecture that you have tried to understand" (qtd. in Elliot 103). Those students considered "less able" would select topics dealing with athletics. A typical writing prompt selected by these students might read: "Some forms of athletics develop character better than others." Elliot reports that results were predictable: "The predictions held true: only one student in one hundred who wrote on athletics obtained a score of 'B' or better. Seventeen students in one hundred, conversely, achieved a grade of 'B' or better who wrote on art" (103). Quoting Sir Philip Hartog, Stalnaker sums up the situation best, asserting that the approach of having students "Write anything about something for anybody" was not sustainable.

Following this report, several of Stalnaker's recommendations for improving reliability were considered, and they were apparently effective. Only two years later, Stalnaker declares a victory over his testing dilemma in "Essay Examinations Reliably Read." Using results from the 1937 College Board report, he asserts that reforms on the levels of uniformity and revisions to writing prompts led to reliability of reading in examinations for "biology, chemistry, English, German, history, Latin, mathematics, physics, and Spanish" (Elliot 104). However, while Stalnaker appears confident that his reforms have yielded desired results, he also points to something else as key to his victory over the problem of assessing essays: creating a sense of cooperation between scholars in the sciences and the humanities. In his "Essay Examinations Reliably Read," he notes:

> Many means are available to improve the reliability of reading, but the results suggest that accurate reading is already being obtained. Cooperation between technician and reader will result in improved procedures which should raise all these reliabilities to even higher figures. However, the present figures indicate consistent reading and should dispel the notion that essay papers can not be read reliably. (672)

The most salient aspect of this passage is Stalnaker's assertion of the importance of creating and sustaining "cooperation between technician and reader." Although Stalnaker desires cooperation between technicians in the sciences and readers in the humanities, he does not see the ends of these two camps as mutually exclusive. In fact, as Elliot notes, Stalnaker specifically anticipates this objection when he remarks on the antagonistic feelings between both camps. "The intensity of these protests," he writes, "makes the groups forget that they are both working toward the same end—an English examination which is sound from every point of view" (qtd. in Elliot 103). From Stalnaker's perspective, the desire for an accurate and reliable assessment of student writing is an end to which all specialties in the university can commit.

Lange, too, is interested in the notion of cooperation. In "What Price English?" he writes: "If we really expect our students to grow in wisdom and in stature as far as the mastery of the language is concerned, all the instructors in *all* classes will have to get behind this project. They will have to get behind it, furthermore, by insisting on 'good' English in all oral discussions and by providing ample opportunity for written work" (426; emphasis added). Lange is convinced that "all the instructors" from "the most inconspicuous half-time laboratory assistant up to the president" may cooperate to enact the project of enforcing the "standards for both written and spoken language" (426). Together, Stalnaker and Lange demonstrate that although the means of writing assessment may become ostensibly more reliable, and the suggestions for reforming freshman composition more specific, the ends toward which these methods are directed remain vague, poorly defined, and invested quite heavily in the literacy myth.

For Thurber, literacy is the aim for composition, one to be achieved in service of the trend toward academic specialization. Manchester's vague understanding of literacy in the contexts of writing, speech, and reading serves to complicate further the very "Sphinx riddle" of composition that he sets out to solve. Finally, Lange believes literacy, and the consequences of possessing it, may be measured and quantified with reliable methods toward indisputable conclusions. His attitude about literacy and assessment leads him to seek "cooperation" at all levels of the university, a consensus about literacy that is unattainable for students and instructors of composition.

Thurber, Manchester, and Lange have in common an abiding belief in the literacy myth. Although it is a belief restricted and complicated by varied and gradually changing circumstances in universities, the solutions proposed by each represents a continuity or legacy of literacy that is endemic to the abolition debate specifically. That is, in one way or another, Thurber, Manchester, and Lange each propose a solution to the problem of freshman English that, in essence, shifts the consequences of confiding in the literacy myth away from composition—the course that seems most invested in the myth itself. Thurber's solution to the "vexing" (9) problem posed by composition involves sharing the responsibility of writing instruction with various disciplines in universities. As such, the burden of meeting the exaggerated expectations of literacy that Thurber possesses becomes the problem of the entire university, not just English. Manchester's insistence on the importance and powers of "extensive reading"—reading that students perform on their own accord and outside of the composition classroom—shifts the responsibility of the most critical component of his solution away from the composition course and into the hands students, not their instructors. Furthermore, Lange's suggestion to eliminate freshman English altogether, in favor of a greater emphasis on composition at the high school levels, is yet another example of shifting the burden of confiding in the literacy myth to anyone besides those charged with the task of teaching it at the university level. In all cases, regardless of where the consequences of confiding in the literacy myth are shifted, the myth remains, and so, too, the perennial problems and complaints about freshman composition.

In my next chapter, I continue my examination of the abolition debate, but I do so with an emphasis on essays that are generally conceded to be making "reformist" rather than "abolitionist" arguments. Similar to Thurber, Manchester, and Lange, the studies discussed in the following chapter have been left out of existing examinations of this debate. Central to my discussion of these studies will be pressing questions about the role of the literacy myth in general and compulsory education more generally: To what extent did the literacy myth specifically play a part in exaggerating the grand rationales that supported compulsory education after the 1930s? In what ways did proposals for reform draw on these exaggerated claims about the consequences of compulsory education and, somewhat paradoxically, contribute to the failure of general education programs? John Guillory notes that "[a]lthough general education constitutes the curriculum that students supposedly have in *common*, the effects of that curriculum tend to be exaggerated or misidentified" ("Who's Afraid of Marcel Proust?" 36). In the next chapter, I demonstrate how the abolition debate may function as a laboratory to explore in more detail the implications of Guillory's statement for proposals that suggest that the compulsory requirement is too important to abolish. Not unlike the abolitionist arguments that they are ostensibly opposed to, these reformist studies rely on similar tendencies to exaggerate the claims and consequences of possessing literacy.

THREE

RECOVERING THE REFORMISTS

Articulating the Educational Reforms of Compulsory Composition

We turn now to several arguments for reform of freshman English from the first half of the twentieth century: "Cannot English departments do something to encourage practical realization of what every teacher admits in theory—that English is fundamental in all studies and in all professions?" Fred A. Dudley poses this and other questions in *The English Journal* in 1929 in an attempt to clarify the purpose of English instruction. He asks: "Can we not convert other teachers to the policy of rewarding well-written and rejecting crudely written papers?" (832). Many years later in "Articulation of the Secondary School and the College," Warner G. Rice notes, "It was during the early thirties, in the blackest of the depression years, that many of us teaching English in the colleges and universities first became actively aware of the need for making a closer connection between our work and that of the secondary schools" (136). Along similar lines and only two years after Rice, in 1940, Alice V. Brower writes in "Problems of High-School English and College Freshman English" that "It would seem that the teacher of college freshman composition should be one of the most superior in the department. So much may be done through this course to help bewildered youth make a better adjustment to college" (730). Finally, in 1961, twenty years after Brower, and in a time marked by what Robert Connors describes as a resurgence of reformist attitudes toward compulsory composition, Thomas S. Kane argues in "Rhetoric and the 'Problem' of Composition" that "What the 'problem' of the writing course finally comes down to, it seems to me, is this: too many of us simply do not know our business. Both in the high school and the university we must begin to take the teaching of composition seriously; in short, to learn the trade and work at it" (505).

I consider in this chapter what historians of writing instruction like Robert Connors have described as the other side of the debate: those interested in reforming freshman English, rather than abolishing it. As in my previous chapter, I am interested in supplementing existing histories of the Great Debate by Greenbaum, Connors, and Russell by examining voices that have been left out or overlooked. That said, I am less interested in discussing why particular voices have been left out than I am in explaining what can be gained by including them and exploring, to some extent, the historical contexts from which they emerge. For example, as I will show, both reformist studies that I examine in this chapter depend on a rhetoric of "cooperation," one that aspires to create more continuity of teaching practices between high school English and freshman composition. Although this rhetoric represents a shared aim for these studies, I show that the emphasis placed on cooperation and continuity is more about persuading students and teachers to ascribe to a particular theory of literacy than it is in developing meaningful reforms of composition instruction. It is, I argue, a better understanding of this specific theory of literacy that is to be gained from examining these overlooked voices of reform.

I begin by examining Alice V. Brower's "Problems of High-School English and College Freshman English" (1942). As a high school English teacher, Brower brings a unique perspective to the debate over compulsory composition. We find, in Brower's spirited essay, evidence of an abiding commitment to the idea that education should be aimed toward the "whole child." This is a sentiment based on her enthusiasm for education that is rooted in scientific findings; the influence of psychology; and progressive-era educational reforms more generally. In her study we also see evidence of the consequences of the rise of private regional associations and committees, both of which gained increasing influence in the 1930s and 1940s because of population growth in the United States and increased enrollments in universities. Accompanying these increased enrollments were calls for greater cooperation and continuity between high schools and colleges. I show how Brower's study relies on this rhetoric of cooperation and continuity as a way to popularize the relevance of progressive reform movements to college composition instructors specifically. My findings have important implications for understanding the unintended consequences of what I call "a rhetoric of cooperation." In Brower's case, even though her rhetoric is aimed toward providing some sense of continuity between high school and colleges, she unintentionally constructs the freshman English course as a site of realizing exaggerated expectations of the consequences of possessing literacy.

Following Brower's study, I examine Warner G. Rice's "Articulation of the Secondary School and the College" (1940). Like Brower, Rice is interested in reforming freshman English by emphasizing cooperation between high school and college-level English instructors. However, the reforms he proposes involve implementing what we might describe as a consulting initiative in which university representatives work with high school instructors to comment on and critique samples of high school essays. Rice's study is noteworthy for several reasons: First, his argument was published in 1940, and as such, precedes his better-known abolitionist sentiments by almost twenty years. By considering the earlier statements of an abolitionist, we get some sense of the thinking behind abolitionism in general. Second, like Brower's study, Rice's essay relies on a rhetoric of cooperation, and although the goals of his inquiry are different from Brower's, both authors share a desire to reform freshman English rather than abolish compulsory composition. By examining how the rhetoric of cooperation functions in these studies and by connecting it to the historical context that created the need for cooperation in the first place, I demonstrate that both Brower and Rice are working toward preserving a view of literacy, one that, above all else, translated into an easily teachable and efficient pedagogy.

In this chapter, I also wish to show that reformists have much in common with abolitionists, especially with respect to the assumptions they make about literacy and the solutions they provide to the ostensible problem of compulsory composition. In doing so, I continue to question the effectiveness of conceptualizing the debate in terms of a reformist/abolitionist divide. Other studies, like Goggin and Miller's "What is *New* About the 'New Abolitionists': Continuities and Discontinuities in the Great Debate," raises similar questions about the terminology used to discuss the debate, but they have done so in ways that lead to further divisions (e.g., abolitionists/"reconc eptualists"). We can better understand why reformists and abolitionists have so much in common by expanding the scope of our examination of these proposals to include larger social, economic, and institutional pressures.

REMEDIES FOR HIGH SCHOOL AND FRESHMAN ENGLISH— "FOR THE GOOD OF US ALL"

One of the first reformist arguments in the 1940s comes from Alice V. Brower, head of the department of English at Davis High School in Mount Vernon, New York. Published in *College English* in 1942, "The Problems of High-School English and College Freshman English" grows out of a presentation Brower gave at the twenty-ninth Annual Meeting of the College Conference on English in the Central Atlantic States. That year the conference met in Atlantic City, and on November 22, 1941, Brower addressed an audience of college teachers of freshman English in hopes of persuading them to see the value of composition at both the high school and college levels.

Brower begins her article by asserting that high school English and college composition teachers have coexisted but lack both a sense of common purpose and a language to articulate their differences in a productive manner. "Seriously," she writes, "this is a very wise step that is being taken today. For so long we have felt a difficulty; now that together we are doing something about it, it would seem a hopeful sign. How much better to be talking *to* and *with* one another instead of *at* and *about*" (725). Brower's italics emphasize her feelings of frustration with the tendency of both high school and college instructors to blame each other for the poor writing of freshman English students. Although Brower is unwilling to accept, on behalf of high schools, the entire burden of the problem, she is motivated by key developments in various fields dedicated to understanding how students learn. For Brower, if these advances are communicated clearly to college instructors, she claims they will function as "remedies for the good of us all" (725).

More specifically, Brower's proposal for reforming the teaching of freshman English is foregrounded in her belief in "practical psychology," which she states is "being applied to the teaching of these high-school girls and boys" (726). According to Brower, developments in psychology in the 1930s and 1940s hold promising implications, especially for understanding students' early childhood development. She writes:

> The factors of age and growth do make for problems of the early years of adolescence that require some techniques and attitudes foreign to the teaching in college years. These must be taken into consideration in any fair discussion. These early years are those of awakening interests on which the high-school teacher must capitalize. (726)

The confidence with which Brower makes her point about the early years of adolescence and the influences of psychology is remarkable, but it is rooted more in the influence of progressive-era education than anything else. In addition, her specific reference to "practical" psychology is further evidence that her instructional methods are devoted to ideals of progressive reform. Contemporary historians of this period have remarked on the connections between practical psychology and progressive-era reforms. For instance, in *American School Reform: Progressive, Equity, and Excellence Movements, 1883–1993*, Michael R. Berube explains, "Progressive education was on the cutting edge of intellectual progress of its time. It was based on rising scientific discoveries, such as biological evolution and the 'new' science of psychology" (14). According to Berube, Margaret Naumberg, a progressive educator and founder of New York's Walden School, would also claim that progressive reforms grew out of "the most recent findings of biology, psychology and education" with the purpose of discovering "ways of redirecting and hammering this vital force of childhood in constructive and creative work" (15). The earnestness with which Brower makes her case for college teachers to recognize the importance of "these early years" is evidence of her own belief in the "vital force of childhood," and it is, I believe, symptomatic of the tone of prevailing pedagogical approaches to writing instruction in high schools during her time.

The progressive era brought us many scholarly studies focusing on the idea of nurturing the whole child and students' psychological development. For instance, in 1902 John Dewey wrote *The Child and the Curriculum*; in 1910, Nathan Oppenheim published *The Development of the Child*; and in 1928 *The Child-Centered School* by Harold Rugg and Ann Schumacher as well as Margaret Naumberg's *The Child and the World* appear (Berube 14). Of particular interest to progressive-era reformers was persuading educators to characterize and understand children as possessing an insatiable longing "to know and be" (Cremin 211). For John Dewey, perhaps the most influential of progressive educators, the perspective presented in Rousseau's *Emile* gave a new meaning to the idea of childhood altogether—as the "time of growing, of developing" in a natural manner (Dewey qtd. in Berube 16). In this way, we can think of the progressive era of educational reform as a time when the notion of childhood possibilities may be considered among other touchstones of the movement: namely, self-expression, creativity, individualism, and pragmatism. At the same time, however, it is also important to acknowledge the repressive and bureaucratic aspects of educational reforms, which are also perceptible in Brower's essay, and discussed later in this chapter.

Childhood, or what Brower repeatedly describes as "these early years" of students, is a critical time of development because "these years are those of awakening interests on which the high-school teacher must capitalize" (726). Although she does not go into detail about what aspects of psychology shed light on the cognitive or intellectual development of children, she is clear about what role English instructors have in this process. "An intense awareness of himself," she writes, "his vocation, his social life, his religious experience, his devotion to his group's activities—all these are paramount in the pupil, and they become an integral part of the high-school teacher's thinking about the pupil" (726). One of the striking aspects of this passage is that Brower's message seems almost insultingly simple: students lead complex lives. But underlying her attempts to change her audience's "thinking about" students is a latent attitude about literacy, and it is one, I argue, that assumes particular benefits from reading.

To a great extent, Brower's characterization of literacy is linked to the qualities she believes a teacher of English must possess, a disposition that must be maintained in the face of a strenuous and taxing teaching load. "With all this," she notes, "one must admit, also, that the daily preparation for teaching these five English classes requires more time and thought to plans and paper-work than do many other subjects" (726). In addition to the responsibility of "sponsoring school clubs, producing the school paper and magazine, planning assembly programs, and commencements," the "good teacher of English" must remain a "most flexible, versatile teacher, always adapting methods and materials to each new" student as well as the "needs and the affairs of the world" (726). Brower also emphasizes the importance of staying abreast of "favorite radio hours," contemporary movie stars, columnists, and theater. After all, she writes, "They are the medium through which the pupils are taught to think, read, write, and speak" (726). In making this point, Brower is urging her audience (which is, again, college English professors) to make their writing courses more relevant to students' needs. But there are other points to be noted about her suggestions. In Brower's opinion, reading poetry above all else is the key to teaching students how to write, think, and speak English appropriately.

> Through the study of poetry, experience is gained in associative thinking and reading. The pupil soon realizes that one gets out of reading what he takes to it. One cannot bring back the wealth of the Indies unless he takes the wealth of the Indies with him. He learns to read for "more than meets the eye" by considering the threefold appeal of poetry to the senses, the emotions, and the intellect. (727)

Underlying her belief in poetry alone to transform students into critical readers—who read for "more than meets the eye"—is a literate bias, one that she attempts to dignify by foregrounding in a curiously ethnocentric proverb, "One cannot bring back the wealth of the Indies unless he takes the wealth of the Indies with him." However, in upholding this adage she undermines, to some extent, her own efforts to complicate prevailing attitudes about students and approaches to college-level writing instruction. By this I mean, Brower's purpose is to persuade her audience to do two things: value students' "early years" and make lectures and assignments more relevant to students' needs. Yet, by situating poetry as the principal site of literacy instruction—in essence, narrowing the path to literacy—and by presuming that the benefits derived from reading alone depend on what students bring to this process, Brower reveals how even the most well-intentioned educational reforms are rendered inconsequential by overly simplistic characterizations and attitudes about literacy. After all, if in the end, learning to speak, write, and read well depends entirely on what students bring to the process, what does it matter if pedagogies are antiquated or out of touch with students' needs?

Among the most remarkable aspects of Brower's comments is how her recommendations for reforming writing instruction reveal how little is known about how students learned during this time.[1] The net result of Brower's recommendations for her audience, I fear, was that she unintentionally reinforced an attitude about students and a characterization of literacy that completely contradicted the educational reforms that were most important to her. In this way, we may think of Brower as sharing much in common with the abolitionists and critics of composition that came before her, especially with respect to the way latent attitudes about literacy restrict the scope of proposed solutions to the problems associated with teaching young writers.

FOR A LIVABLE WORLD TOMORROW

In the second part of her proposal, Brower draws on a report by the Westchester County Association of Teachers of English (WCATE), of which she was the chair. "For several years," she writes, "this group has been seeking acquaintance with college methods in the hope of effecting smoother articulation" (728). With the aim of "perfecting the preparation of high school pupils in English," the WCATE examined reports from former high school students as well as professional publications. The committees' conclusions, and the tone with which Brower communicates their findings, are provocative:

> I shall have to say that as a group you, too, show a wide range of individual differences—so wide that you create for the high-school teacher an almost impossible task. We could not begin to satisfy all of you. We could never expect 100 per cent uniformity, but we do wish that you had some small semblance of it, some organization that voiced more of your policies. With all of our good intentions and attention to detail of techniques of reading and composition, pupils return with varying tales of experience. (728)

This report is important to consider here because Brower uses the findings to highlight how little continuity exists at the college level with respect to the type of instruction students receive in composition. For instance, Brower states that two former students—one with an "above-the-average" rating and the other with a "below-the-average" rating—attended the same university, but ended up in two different English classes. To the committee's surprise, the below-average student received a higher grade than the above-average student. Dismayed by this report, and with "no other motive than to learn,"

Brower notes that the committee then began asking "for samples of corrected Freshman papers" (729) from English instructors. "I am embarrassed," she writes, "to tell you what the committee found on some of those papers. They did not help us much; in truth they confused and disturbed us" (729). As an example, Brower includes the following excerpt from a comment by a college-level instructor on one of these papers. It reads:

> The preparation in English sounds good; but I know those small New York high schools; they are nothing but Regents' machines; and once the syllabus is covered, to hell with anything else! Her judgment is very bad, e.g., she thinks she was well prepared in writing but read a page of this and you will see why she gets D's all the time. The poor girl will never do better. Incidentally, she wants to major in English. God help us! (729).

Although Brower is concerned that college English instructors seem to lack a continuity of teaching practices as well as reliable and consistent methods of assessment, she seems most disturbed by the characterization of students that may be evinced from such comments. Brower advocates an alternative approach. The freshman English instructor must possess a "love of youth itself" (730).

This view of students—and of youth more generally—is a quintessential part of progressive-era approaches to education. And without this predisposition, Brower feels the course in freshman composition fails to achieve its ultimate purpose. The importance of valuing and characterizing students as children "in a state of grace" is most evident in the conclusion of her article when she presents, as evidence, the letter of a first-grade teacher, who at the end of the first week of classes wrote letters to the parents of his students.

> My Dear Mr. Armstrong:
>
> I thank you for lending me your little child today. All the years of love and care and training which you have given him have stood him in good stead in his work and in his play. I send him home to you tonight, I hope a little stronger, a little taller, a little freer, a little nearer his goal. Lend him to me again tomorrow, I pray you. In my care of him I shall show my gratitude. (734)

To be sure, Brower closes with this anecdote to appeal to her audience on an emotional level, but also to emphasize the importance of the progressive ideals of childhood in her vision for reforming writing instruction. Rightly sensing that the letter from a first-grade teacher will not be enough to persuade her audience that progressive ideals are relevant to instruction at the college level, she extends the anecdote even further, and somewhat predictably, makes strong connections to issues of literacy. "But they are the same boys and girls," she writes, "children of parents who for longer years have loved and nurtured them and looked with proud anticipation to the years of their college fulfillment with you. . . . Yours is the final chance to equip them with that mystic power of utterance, of communication . . . that may give tongue to philosophies that will transform the chaos of today into a livable world for their tomorrow!" (734).

To a great extent Brower's final statement constructs the freshman English course as a site of realizing exaggerated expectations of the consequences of possessing literacy. The notion that the course creates the conditions and the type of students who can "transform the chaos of today into a livable world for their tomorrow" raises the possibility that for reformist arguments, the need to exaggerate the claims of literacy is similar to that of abolitionists. As I demonstrated in my second chapter, Thurber, Manchester, and Lange all overstate the significance of literacy in their proposals to abolish freshman English. For abolitionists, one effect of such exaggerated expectations is that they translate into unreasonable expectations for composition as well. In Brower's study, we see a similar tendency, and the consequence for her study is the same: confiding in myths of literacy leads her to develop unattainable learning outcomes and expectations for freshman English. Furthermore, Brower's exaggerated expectations are indicative of something equally as complex as her attitudes about literacy. Her belief in composition's ability to "transform the chaos of today into a livable world for [students'] tomorrow" (734) is reminiscent of concerns articulated by nineteenth-century school promoters supporting compulsory education.

Michael Katz notes that, "nineteenth-century school promoters argued that public education would alleviate five problems: crime and poverty, cultural heterogeneity, poor work habits, 'idle youth,' and the anxieties of middle-class parents about their children's future" (*Reconstructing American Education* 115). If this is the case, we may understand Brower to be appropriating, to some extent, the rhetoric of nineteenth-century public school promoters to persuade college English teachers to realize the import and relevance of compulsory composition. Although she does not argue that composition will reduce crime or poverty, she clearly possesses apprehension about the future for her students. This is important to note because, as Katz asserts, overstating the significance of compulsory schooling did not help it realize its aims. "Despite school promoters' rhetoric," he explains, "public education had very little effect on crime, delinquency, and poverty, which did not disappear or even significantly diminish" (115). In fact, little to no connection was perceptible between the amount of public education and the extent of "distress and disorder in social life" (115). We know from Connors, Greenbaum, and Russell that the "tradition of complaint"—comprised of attempts to both reform and abolish composition—began with composition's inception and, as I will show in my final chapter, continues today with little to no effect. When we consider Brower's essay in the context of this long line of proposals for reforming and abolishing composition, we may understand her study as a response to what she perceives as the "chaos of today," and also, to an even greater extent, as a means of coping with the failure of high schools and colleges to live up to the expectations that they have set for themselves.

Brower, however, was not alone in holding such high expectations for high school and freshman English; in fact, historians like Katz contend that this is a trait endemic to American educational reforms more generally. In Katz's view, "exactly why Americans have placed such a trust in formal schooling remains far from clear" alongside "the disillusionment that periodically arises when a new generation discovers that schools cannot fulfill the mission with which they have been entrusted" (124). Educators have responded to this disillusionment by developing what Katz describes as a "repertoire of strategies for coping with failure" (124). In some cases, educators have blamed learning problems on students. In other cases the fault was placed with particular methods or the "quality of instruction" (124). In Brower's case, we find her blaming the process by which students articulate from high school to college composition, as well as the failure of college English instructors to prioritize pedagogical approaches that are consistent with progressive-era reforms. Above all, however, Brower's essay should be of interest to teacher-researchers in composition because of how the rhetoric she employs demonstrates that exaggerated attitudes about literacy are ever-present, even in attempts to reform composition with the best intentions. Furthermore, as we have learned, such attitudes seem to perpetuate the tendency to overstate the significance of composition at both the high school and college levels.

In the following section, I examine another proposal for reforming freshman English, Warner G. Rice's "Articulation of the Secondary School and the College." Similar to Brower's study, Rice's essay speaks to the tendency of composition reformers to rely on the rhetoric of cooperation in the hopes of creating some sense of continuity between high school and college English courses. Given that the following study is followed twenty years later by Rice's own critique of compulsory composition, I believe it is especially important to examine the rhetoric of this study. In doing so, we get some sense of the development of Rice's thinking about what he perceives to be at the root of the problem with freshman English.

To clarify: in chapter 2, I briefly discussed Rice's 1959 NCTE address, a presentation that was eventually published in *College English* in 1960 as "A Proposal for the Abolition of Freshman English, As It Is Now Commonly Taught, from the College Curriculum." Rice argues that composition should only have a place at the high school levels. In this article, his complaints about freshman English are very familiar, especially when considered in the context of the abolition debate: students are inept; instructors are intellectually unprepared to the course; the writing and reading skills necessary for college should be required before admission to college. Because his objections and critiques of composition are so consistent with other abolitionists, it is not surprising that he plays a prominent role in Greenbaum's, Connors's, and Russell's histories of the abolition debate. However, twenty years before his NCTE address, Rice articulates a different opinion on the problem of freshman English, one he expresses in an argument that is clearly reformist in nature.

THE FAILURE OF HIGH-SCHOOL COMPOSITION: A "SILVER LINING IN A VERY DARK CLOUD"

In "Articulation of the Secondary School and the College," Rice is explicitly interested in persuading readers to become "actively aware of the need for making a closer connection" (136) between colleges and high schools. Ultimately, Rice's study deals with the "new demands" placed upon the freshman English course, demands that grew out of increased enrollments during the 1930s. During this period, Rice remarks that English instructors are becoming increasingly aware of the importance of students' transition between secondary and post-secondary institutions (136). This epiphany was triggered among the faculty of the University of Michigan by "very badly prepared" freshman English students coming from high schools. The opportunity to deal with the problem of freshman English at its perceived source—poor instruction at the high school level—leads Rice to proclaim optimistically: "Very likely this is one of the patches of silver lining in a very dark cloud." Without a doubt, this statement's tenor suggests that Rice holds some hope for reforming composition during this time, but to understand why this is and to have some sense of the pressures that Rice is responding to, we must explore the historical context from which his study emerges.

Although the Great Depression led to many negative externalities (including declining birthrates and reduced expenditures for municipal initiatives) one of the most remarkable developments of the 1930s was the increase in enrollments at the college *and* high school levels. Lawrence Cremin reports that secondary enrollments rose from 4,800,000 in 1929–30 to 7,100,000 in 1939–40 (274). With increased enrollments came an increasingly diverse student body, one "readily receptive to reform" (274). In such a climate, Cremin writes, "it was almost inevitable that the polyglot system of ideas, assumptions, and practices called progressive education would continue to exert profound influence" (274); thus, the influence of progressive education was perceptible in a number of ways: In addition to increased enrollments in high schools, kindergartens and nursery schools also experienced growth (306). As such, curricula were reorganized at all levels, creating opportunities for work in agriculture and home economics, as well as the arts (306). Reforms on the curricular level created opportunities for "cocurricular" or "extracurricular" involvement, so that by the 1930s and 1940s student clubs and other activities were mainstays in American schools (306). Related to some extent to curricular reforms, classroom practices changed on several levels. Cremin reports that "students and teachers alike tended to be more active, more mobile, and more informal in their relationships with one another" (307).

As educators began to draw on the latest research in psychology, learning, and other theories of childhood development, the materials used for instruction also transformed: textbooks became more attractive, and teachers began incorporating other devices and heuristics like flash cards and local flora in the classroom (307). In general, state certification requirements became increasingly popular, leading to "better educated" instructors and professional courses that reflected the aims of progressive education. In addition, the architecture of schools was adapted to account for increased enrollments and the influence of curricular reforms with progressive aims. Among other changes, schools were modified to include assembly rooms, playgrounds, miniature tables and chairs, movable furniture and partitions, as well as improved lighting and ventilation (307). Cremin suggests that such architectural modifications to schools lent progressive reforms "a measure of permanence" (307). In sum, these changes point to a period of reform marked by considerable variations in teaching approaches with a gradual shift in pedagogical focus from teacher-centered classrooms to more student-centered instruction.

It is in this context of diverse educational reforms and in a culture marked by conflicts over competing visions of the function of secondary schools that Rice argues for stronger cooperation between high schools and colleges. On the surface, this argument makes a lot of sense, especially given its timing and Rice's position as elected chairman of the College Section of the National Council of Teachers of English. However, the type of cooperation that Rice had in mind did not involve curricular reforms in the college English classroom. In fact, Rice seems most interested in creating "greater continuity and effectiveness" and "something like uniform preparation" at the high school level (137).

At their base, Rice's suggestions are an extension of recommendations put forth by the Michigan Committee on the Articulation of High School and College English in their *Preparation for College English: An Interpretation of College Entrance Standards in English* (1935). Under their plan, high school teachers submitted their students' papers to members of the Department of English at the University of Michigan. Rice refers to the readers of these high school essays as "consultants" (139), charged with the task of analyzing and evaluating any written work submitted, "in terms of its fitness to meet University standards for entering freshman" (140).

Rice suggests that oversight of this process indicated that the consultants' comments and criticisms "adhered to standards that are remarkably constant" (140). These standards specifically informed the recommendations for writing instruction that the department provided for incoming students; namely, that students in the eleventh and twelfth grades "should be warned away from fine writing, extravagant fantasy, high-flown rhetoric" and restricted to subjects with which they had some familiarity so that they might "write clearly, accurately, and logically" (141). The committee's recommendations speak to the possibility that the essays they read helped to form the suggestions they provided. In other words, not all standards were in place before consultants began evaluating essays from high schools. Rice repeatedly suggests that the point of the consulting initiative was to inform high school instructors and students of the "standards" (140) universities have in place to evaluate writing. Yet, he admits that the criteria used for evaluating student writing were "developed largely through careful consideration of the evidence that came in the high school papers read—that is, they were not established on a priori considerations" (141). Despite this fact (or perhaps because of it), Rice claimed that the consulting initiative was a resounding success, so much so that he suggested that the plan should be "extended to the work of other departments—mathematics, history, foreign languages" (144). If this is the case, then Rice's belief in the effectiveness of the consulting initiative reveals more about why the program was in place than about the quality of writing being submitted for review.

Interestingly, the type of evidence that Rice provides to demonstrate the effectiveness of the Michigan Committee's effectiveness shares similarities with the evidence that Brower presents in her study to remark on the *ineffectiveness* of consulting programs between high schools and colleges. Like Brower's study, Rice's essay relies on letters and feedback from high school teachers and administrators attesting to the effectiveness of the program. "The work of our consultants," Rice writes, "has been rewarded by grateful and (to us) gratifying letters from many of the high schools which sent in student themes." One letter, written by the principal of a secondary school, reads:

> I am indeed favorably impressed by the co-operative experiment conducted by the English Department at the University. I was greatly pleased with your analysis of the samples of composition which we sent. Your plans for conducting the project another year meet with my hearty approval. (141)

Another letter, written by a high school teacher, not only testifies to the usefulness of the program but also seeks feedback for further curriculum development:

> Your careful criticism of my 11th grade papers proved so interesting to my 12th grade classes that they begged me to send you some of their work . . . For several years we have tried to give our seniors some experience in thesis writing. They follow a procedure outlined in their text, with drill on hunting down material, taking notes on cards, organizing an outline, etc., the teacher checking the work at each stage. I allow them to correlate this work with that done in other courses, if they wish, and I permit any who use a typewriter to type the final draft. We should like your opinion as to whether this is a useful type of assignment for those preparing for college. (141)

The success and excitement with which Rice discusses his consultant plan is curious given Brower's experience with a similar initiative. After all, according to Brower (who again was a high school English teacher), college composition instructors possess a regressive view of students. They are overly concerned with instilling taste and judgment, rely too heavily on rote memorization and drill and, above all, do not possess a love of youth itself. However, despite their differences, the extraordinary thing about Brower's and Rice's studies is that they parallel each other in a significant way: both of their proposed reforms are linked directly to the University of Michigan's *Preparation for College English.*

In the conclusion of her address to college composition instructors, Brower notes: "I do believe that much could be done to help a larger number of teachers throughout the country if more concrete material were published by your organization, similar to that prepared by the University of Michigan, entitled *Preparation for College English*" (732). In the end, then, despite her reservations and concerns about the articulation of students from high schools to colleges she is, like Rice, convinced that the University of Michigan has figured something out with respect to the problem of freshman English. When Brower's and Rice's studies are compared, the language and effects of progressive-era reforms are certainly perceptible. Brower possesses an abiding belief in the value of educating the "whole child," and it is one that she desires freshman English instructors to possess. Rice is responding to a period marked by conflicts over competing visions of the purpose and value of progressive-era reforms. In both studies, the authors identify the ideals of cooperation and continuity as key solutions to the problem of freshman English. However, when we examine the evidence that they have in common—the Michigan's Committee's analysis of student writing—we find inclinations toward social order and control manifested in a desire to develop efficient pedagogy above all else. With an eye on this preoccupation with efficiency, I turn, in the following section, to two of the seventeen sample essays discussed in *Preparation for College English*. One is rated "Very Bad" and the other "Acceptable." The committee's analysis of these themes sheds light on the way attitudes about literacy overlap with the report's overarching commitment to the principles of attainment and decency, which previous studies of reformist arguments do not address. My analysis also reveals potential reasons why reformist arguments in the 1940s failed, and why it may be unrealistic to expect that educational structures may be reformed to serve different goals than those they were originally intended to achieve.

PREPARATION FOR COLLEGE ENGLISH: CONTINUITY, ATTAINMENT, AND DECENCY

While *Preparation for College English* was first published in 1935, it was revised in 1942. The latter version represents a more comprehensive statement of the Michigan Committee's suggestions for preparing secondary school students who were bound for college. The revised report is broken down into four sections, including a "General Statement," a section on "Language and Composition," "Reading and Literature," and finally a list of "Reference Books for Teachers of High-School Literature." Almost thirty post-secondary institutions from Michigan and beyond participated in the "Michigan Project on The Articulation of High-School and College English.[2] The participants, representatives of many colleges and consultants, were placed on two subcommittees, one for "Language and Composition," and the other for "Reading and Literature." All themes were rated according to their "acceptability, with an analysis showing the bases upon which the ratings were made" (18). From the perspective of the bulletin's authors, because the themes they analyzed were "the work of freshman in their first week at college," the samples exemplify the quality of writing from students just finishing high school. Given the number of schools involved in the articulation project as well as the number of themes analyzed in the publication, we may understand the ratings and analysis of these essays to represent with some accuracy the nature of writing instruction being provided for students in Michigan and its surrounding areas during this time.

The authors note that most themes discussed in the bulletin were "written as impromptus." Pupils chose from a list of topics provided by the instructor and were given one hour to complete the assignment. The readers of themes were asked to mark and evaluate themes based on a list of eleven criteria, touching on everything from "development of argument" to "acceptable English." Finally, readers were asked to evaluate each paper as "Excellent," "Acceptable," "Not Acceptable," or "Very Bad" (20).

The following paper received a rating of "Very Bad" and is quoted in full below:

Radio, Best Source of News

> The radio, one of our more modern inventions, is the best means we have for securing news. Now take the war over in London, if it (weren't) wasn't for the radio we could not receive our news as rapidly as we do. For the accuracy of the radio it may be said it is as good as our other means of news, for it is all censured before it comes to us. Then to in reporting the news, the reporter can be right at the seen of the news happing, he can put more "unph" into the story whereas if one were writing it for the paper "we" would have to wait until they had set up type, possible for an extra. This goes to show that speed is the thing in this modern day and age.
>
> The radio has helped in more (cases) ways then one to save the (life) lives of some people. Take for instance thee airplane, it is a means of radio, it contacts people who are involved and helps to give us news when on of our modern passenger planes are in trouble, it to helps to save the people who are in trouble, it passes on to the receiver the location of its misshap an away goes help to the people, and more news for the people who are home waiting to hear if there beloved ones (is) are safe or injured.
>
> This goes to show the importance of the radio (1) in relationship to man an its troubled ones or I might say to man and its public through out the world. There is no end to the possibilities the radio has in making this world safer to live in. (21)

According to the analysis provided by readers, the essay is "hardly competent" and indicative of a writer who is "plainly lacking in the essential means of organizing his ideas for communication" (21). The first paragraph "dismisses summarily points of enough importance" (21) that they would warrant more complete explication in separate paragraphs. The second paragraph introduces ideas of "doubtful relevance" (21), and the third paragraph proceeds to a conclusion unrelated to the idea articulated in the beginning of the paper. To be sure, readers identify other "major weaknesses" (21). "Errors and faults of style abound," they write; "They include violation of concord, bad diction, awkward and occasionally incoherent sentences, and more than one example of plain obscurity" (21). In sum, the evaluative comments and criticisms by readers may be described as concerned primarily with formal aspects of composition with particular interest in grammar, organization, and style.

The emphasis placed on the finished product as well as the complete disregard for the writing process of students is a classic indicator of what contemporary composition and rhetoric scholars have termed "current-traditional rhetoric." Robert Connors connects English instructors' penchant for fixating on the formal features of composition to a "single-minded enforcement of standards of mechanical and grammatical correctness in writing" ("The Rhetoric of Mechanical Correctness" 72). In her entry for "Current-Traditional Rhetoric" in the *Encyclopedia of Rhetoric and Composition: Communication from Ancient Times to the Information Age*, Sharon Crowley connects the practice to the British rhetorical tradition "located in Lockean empiricism but tinctured with a dose of Scottish commonsense realism" (156). In a similar vein, Nan Johnson's *Nineteenth-Century Rhetoric in North America* traces the progenitors of current-traditional thought and its influence on "formal instruction in oral and written communication" (3) to George Campbell's *Philosophy of Rhetoric* (1776), Hugh Blair's *Lectures on Rhetoric and Belles Lettres* (1783), and Alexander Bain's *English Composition* (1866).

Whereas Connors, Crowley, and Johnson offer convincing arguments for the presence of current-traditional impulses in formal writing instruction, the Michigan Committee's concluding remarks about "Radio, The Best Source of News" lead me to believe that attitudes and implications of literacy are also significant during this time. Of the essay's style and organization, they assert that the "most serious" faults of the paper "are the numerous and frequently inexcusable misspellings" (21). According to the authors, these indicate "fundamentally bad attitudes" (21) and contribute to a "total accumulation of errors, toward producing an impression of illiteracy" (21). Above all, in embracing and implementing the suggestions and views of the committee, a way of instructing students that allows them to avoid the appearance of illiteracy is what is most at stake. During the 1940s, this task was made increasingly difficult by growing enrollments and an increasingly diverse student body.

Let us return to Lawrence Cremin's report that secondary school enrollments rose from 4,800,000 in 1929–30 to 7,100,000 in 1939–40. Postsecondary enrollments increased significantly during this time as well, with roughly 1.5 million students attending universities in the 1940s. In the context of these institutional pressures, we may read the motivations and recommendations of the Michigan Committee in a different light, especially when we remember that their plight was nothing new in the history of composition. After all, Sharon Crowley remarks in *The Methodical Memory: Invention in Current-Traditional Rhetoric* that the composition course itself "was invented out of whole cloth in response to late nineteenth-century hysteria about the low levels of literacy manifested by entering college students" (141).

With the increased interest in the articulation of students from high schools to colleges, the authors of *Preparation for College English* are responding to similar concerns. Rising enrollments coupled with perennial complaints about low levels of literacy and a demand for a cadre of instructors devoted to the teaching of composition created a need for instructional materials that could be delivered to students *and* instructors in the most efficient way possible. However, in the early 1940s, World War II also provided further impetus for educational "innovations" seeking greater cooperation, continuity, and efficiency. Between 1941 and 1945, the government put 16,354,000 men in uniform, and almost 10 million entered the draft (Elliot 117). In 1942, the same year that *Preparation for College English* was published, the *Forty-Second Annual Report of the Executive Secretary* of the College Entrance Examination Board announced: "Broad plans for greater co-operation in the future between school and college need not be discarded, but these should be put in the background. Every effort must now be centered on the present with help for the war effort as the paramount concern" (qtd, in Elliot 117). Evidence of this growing concern for the war effort is clear in both the thematic focus of the following essay and, as I argue, in the analysis provided by the Michigan Committee. The following sample and analysis by the Michigan Committee is also indicative of their commitments toward building greater cooperation between high school English and college composition. The theme received a rating of "Acceptable" and is quoted in full below.

A Freshman Looks at Conscription

> Conscription comes to America in a time of dire need. Out of the chaos in Europe is rising a powerful military machine threatening the remaining democracies with absolute ruin. Between us and immediate invasion stands the power and might of the British—their fleet and air force.
>
> It need be said that we are not prepared in this case of threatened invasion. Americans are altogether too sure of our military strength, which in reality is a mere nothing to what it should be.

> It's true that there is not equipment enough to service all of the men that will be trained in military tactics though conscription. But is it not infinitely better to have the training with which to use the equipment when it is ready?
>
> The people in America today who best appreciate the need of military training for our men are the army experts, who know what may happen and grant that it is very possible. Their job, of course, is to impress this into the minds of the people.
>
> Conscription is a very necessary thing to the Army and Navy. It is the only way that our military weaknesses can be filled in and strengthened.
>
> Many, many women (most of them mothers) are forming anti-conscription leagues, nor can you blame them for not wanting their sons endangered by war. But which is better, sacrificing democracy or making human sacrifices to save that democracy?
>
> Now you enter the field of violent argument. The plea of anguished mothers on one side, and the plea of democracy for rescue on the other. It is merely a measure to insure our safety and to protect ourselves in case any foreign military power threaten us.
>
> Can conscription really hurt us? Will it send our manhood to its death? No, at this time it can be but a preparatory measure for such a time when it's needed. Conscription does come at a time of dire need, the need of bolstering our democracy at its most critical period. (28)

Although the final judgment of the committee is favorable, what exactly students and teachers should learn from this sample is difficult to discern, partly because the committee's explanation of their "acceptable" rating begins with a discussion of the principal shortcomings of the essay. "The chief fault," they write, "is over-paragraphing" (28). They assert that the "loosely connected paragraphs indicate slipshod thinking" (28), and that the paragraphs comprising the "body of the paper are presented in a sketchy and desultory manner" (28). For instance, readers were particularly critical of the pupil's claim about the American military lacking strength. They write: "Instead of presenting evidence and developing the point, the writer leaves it as a mere assertion and makes a new start in a third and only remotely related paragraph which attempts to answer one of the early objections to conscription" (28). From the readers' view, the overall lack of development and "slipshod thinking" contribute to an essay by which "No reader is likely to be convinced" (28). The authors advocate a thorough revision of the essay, one that would transform the pupil's work into a single "well-developed paragraph calling for conscription as a military necessity" (28). Such a revision, they argue, would be more convincing to readers than the "four feeble and poorly connected paragraphs" (28).

Given the bulletin's statement that the purpose and function of these sample essays is to provide acceptable models of college level writing for high school students, the analysis raises a critical question: If the essay is indicative of poor thinking, lacks development because of poor paragraph construction, and is ultimately unconvincing, why did reviewers give it an "acceptable" rating? Although the student needs "training in paragraph and organization," they write, "In terms of mechanics, the paper is acceptable" (28). According to the readers the essay demonstrates facility with "grammar, sentence structure, spelling, punctuation, idiom, and matters of a like nature" (28). Much as in the previous student essay, then, concerns about formal aspects of writing are the most important to readers, and even though "A Freshman Looks at Conscription" misses its mark entirely, offering an unpersuasive and underdeveloped argument, the essay is still held up as an acceptable model for high school students to imitate and for instructors to teach. One reason for this, I argue, is an underlying motivation for *Preparation for College English*: to provide a solution to the problem of overworked composition instructors. This solution comes in the form of a pedagogical approach to writing instruction that emphasizes mechanical correctness above all other concerns.

In *Composition-Rhetoric: Backgrounds, Theory, and Pedagogy*, Robert Connors demonstrates that at the post-secondary level, pedagogies emphasizing mechanical correctness have long been a solution to increased enrollments and the ostensible problems imposed by illiteracy. In fact, Connors connects the rise of "mechanical-correctness standards in Composition" to the 1880s, when the first freshman English courses emerged. "Most teachers," he writes, "were responsible for teaching between 140 and 200 students" (140). At Yale's Sheffield Scientific School, for example, one professor and instructor were responsible for correcting the themes and compositions of over 250 students; in addition, English instructors at this institution were also responsible for grading the compositions for three upper-level courses for a total of over 300 students (140). Connors reports that at the University of Chicago, "which prided itself on its small classes, the course in 'required theme-writing' averaged over 65 students per class" (140). Certainly, the rise of and obsession with mechanical correctness was a response to the perceived illiteracy crisis created by new college students in the 1880s, but it was also a means for teachers to "deal with their huge stacks of student themes" (142). Histories of writing instruction by Applebee, Brereton, Berlin, Connors, and Crowley all attest to the fact that by the 1940s the focus placed on mechanical correctness dominated prevailing approaches to writing instruction. As we have seen, not much is novel or innovative about the Michigan Committee's recommendations or their motivations for reform. Concerns about the illiteracy of incoming freshman English students and the fixation on mechanical correctness as a solution to the problem of illiteracy have, in many respects, defined composition pedagogy since its inception.

However, we may view the rhetoric of cooperation and continuity in these reformist arguments as representing a shared interest, not so much in developing meaningful or innovative composition instruction, but in persuading teachers and students to ascribe to a particular theory of literacy that, at heart, translates into easily teachable and efficient pedagogy. Sharon Crowley remarks in *The Methodical Memory* that "current-traditional rhetoric," which is precisely the type of writing instruction that the Michigan Committee is advocating, has "very little to do with learning to write." She asserts: "Just as its initial success was stimulated by institutional needs, its continued maintenance by the academy has a good deal more to do with institutional circumstances than it does with the appropriateness of its theory of discourse for writing instruction" (147). Taken together, I believe Brower, Rice, and *Preparation for College English* are supported by an abiding belief in freshman English's capacity to realize the promises of the literacy myth, hopes rooted in instilling students with the appearances of competency and decency specifically. Yet because of institutional pressures brought on by exploding enrollments—pressures complicated further by competing visions for implementing various educational reforms—their recommendations are merely restatements of antiquated precepts intended to preserve the status and place of the literacy myth in post-secondary education.

As Michael Katz notes in *The Irony of Early School Reform*, the implications of developing educational reforms along the lines of shared interests, like the literacy myth, are significant. He writes: "Here, then, is another danger. When educational reform becomes too bound up with personal and group interests, it loses the capacity for self-criticism. It can be a dazzling diversionary activity turning heads away from the real nature of social problems. It can become a vested interest in its own right, so pious and powerful that it can direct public scorn to anyone who doubts" (217). The reformists discussed in this chapter are "too bound up" with a shared interest in the literacy myth. Furthermore, Brower's belief in the importance of constructing students as children "in a state of grace" blinds her to the normative impulses of progressive-era reforms. Similarly, both Rice and Brower's confidence in the recommendations outlined in *Preparation for College English* reveals how unaware they were of the fact that the reforms espoused by the committee were not reforms at all, but rather restatements of mainstays of composition pedagogy intended to function as temporary stop gaps for coping with increased enrollments at both the high school and college levels.

Taken together, these reformist essays are examples of scholars pursuing poorly defined problems with mismatched solutions. In "Reforming Again, Again, and Again," Larry Cuban notes, "It is important to policymakers, practitioners, administrators, and researchers to understand why reforms return but seldom substantially alter the regularities of schooling. The risks involved with a lack of understanding include pursuing problems with mismatched solutions, spending energies needlessly, and accumulating despair" (11). Existing histories of the abolition debate demonstrate that proposals for abolishing composition also occur again, again, and again. However, it is worthwhile to examine the chief rationales and motivations that constitute the rhetoric of both composition abolitionists and reformers. What we find is that arguments on both sides of the debate demonstrate a tendency both to overstate the significance of literacy—specifically the literary view of literacy—and to formulate unattainable expectations for the composition course. Recognizing that these expectations are inextricably linked to vague definitions and characterizations of literacy as well as literacy myths specifically is a critical part of understanding why both abolitionists and reformists have failed. It seems that both Brower and Rice simply expected too much of literacy, of freshman composition students and teachers, and of the reforms they wished to put into place. In Rice's case, the consequences of such expectations resulted in the accumulation of his own despair, culminating in his proposal to abolish freshman English almost two decades after his reformist study. My examination of Rice's plan raises the rather striking possibility that abolitionism has its roots in a place we might least suspect—in failed attempts to reform composition. If this is the case, teacher-researchers in composition would do well to remember that although the tenor and tone of reformist studies are more subdued (and perhaps less compelling) than the claims and rhetoric that define abolitionist critiques, the stakes of studies committed to reforming the teaching of writing may be higher than once thought. After all, if failed proposals for reforming composition, in essence, set the stage for abolitionist critiques down the road, then what is at stake in reforming the teaching of writing may be the existence of the course itself—not simply creating better writers, more prepared teachers, or instilling the appearance of literacy in our students.

With this possibility in mind, I argue that it is important to understand the reasons for particular reform proposals' failures in the past; as Larry Cuban notes, "such questions about why reforms failed in the past and why they return go to the heart of present policy debates . . ." (3). Thus, I turn in my next chapter to a more contemporary example of the debate over compulsory composition, Sharon Crowley's 1998 proposal to abolish the "universal requirement" of composition. In turning to a contemporary example of abolitionism, I do not mean to suggest that the composition-reformist era extends from Brower and Rice in the 1940s to Crowley in the 1990s. As Norbert Elliot and Robert Connors indicate in their histories of writing instruction, proposals both for reforming and abolishing composition subsided during the late 1940s, as scholars turned to support the war effort. However, by the late 1950s we see a resurgence of abolitionism with the publication of Warner G. Rice's "A Proposal for the Abolition of Freshman English" in 1959 (Connors 287). With the slow growth of composition studies as a field in the early 1960s, we enter another period of reformism in which composition scholars worked enthusiastically to explore connections between the precepts of classical rhetoric and composition pedagogy. Robert Connors notes that we see a slight increase in abolitionism in the late 1960s and early 1970s (R. M. Hoover published her "Taps for Freshman English?" in 1974); however, between 1975 and 1990 we find no proposals for the general abolition of the composition course. Certainly, Crowley's proposal for abolishing compulsory composition is noteworthy because it emerges after a relatively prolonged and quiet period in the debate over compulsory composition. More significantly, however, when Crowley asserts her position she is doing so, in the words of Robert Connors, as a composition "insider" (292). Of composition insiders, Robert Connors writes, "they can make their case from within the discourse of the field rather than complaining scornfully from without, as most abolitionists have done in the past" (292). If this is true, then Crowley's abolitionist position strikes at the heart of contemporary debates over composition in unique ways. In examining Crowley's position in the debate over the effectiveness and aims of compulsory composition, we may gain a better understanding of the arguments that have helped to delineate the boundaries of contemporary composition studies.

FOUR

IN THIS SPIRIT

The Rhetoric of Referencing a Current and Traditional Complaint

> In this spirit, I offer a modest proposal. Let's abolish the universal requirement. Let's just stop insisting that every student who enrolls in a two-year college or four-year university must take a required composition course.
>
> —Sharon Crowley, *Composition in the University*

> A writer cannot simply present another's words without valuing them, valorizing or denigrating them, even in direct quotation. Every act of reporting discourse—relating another's words as "direct," "indirect," or "quasi-direct" discourses in Volosinov's terminology—carries with it stylistic, rhetorical, and ideological consequences.
>
> —Kay Halasek, *A Pedagogy of Possibility*

In *Composition in the University: Historical and Polemical Essays* (1998), Sharon Crowley delineates many reasons to abolish compulsory composition. One of her most compelling points grows out of her concern about the relationship between composition and myths of literacy. Specifically, she believes that popular conceptions of the powers of literacy and the pedagogical capabilities of composition are exaggerated. "The myth of the academic essay," she writes, "continues to nurture massive Freshman English programs for reasons other than its salience to writing instruction" (233). For Crowley, freshman English "fosters and supports" what she describes as the "American belief" in universal standards of literacy (233), standards that Crowley believes are unattainable. She asks: "Can we impart literacy in a quarter or a semester or a year? What is literacy, anyhow? And whose literacy do we teach?" (234). Questions like these demonstrate the singularity of Crowley's abolitionist stance within the "Tradition of Complaint." Not only is her study distinct because it is written by what Robert Connors terms a "composition insider," it also touches on concerns about literacy's definition and fundamental nature. Consequently, in this chapter, I am less interested in explicating the assumptions that Crowley makes about literacy. She readily admits that the field of composition needs to address assumptions about the powers of literacy and its role in the teaching of composition. Instead, I argue that we must look more closely at how, when, where, and why scholars in composition refer to Crowley's polemic. I have two goals in this chapter: first, by closely examining citations of Crowley's proposal, I hope to gain a more complete understanding of how and why her abolitionist stance has come to stand in for the entire "Tradition of Complaint" in contemporary composition scholarship. And second, knowing that Crowley's participation in the Great Debate grows out of her concern over pressures imposed by and questions about ambiguous definitions of literacy, I hope to demonstrate the extent to which the various ways scholars reference Crowley's polemic both elide and, in some cases, make more explicit the nuance of her position with respect to attitudes about literacy.

What follows, then, is a discussion of both the subtleties of Crowley's position on the first-year requirement as well as an overview of how citation systems have potentially impacted the reception of and position of Crowley's polemic in the Great Debate over compulsory composition. These topics warrant extended discussions for different reasons. Crowley's call for the abolition of the first-year requirement has a somewhat controversial status in composition, a position achieved by numerous references to her work. A search using Google Scholar reveals that Crowley's *Composition in the University* was cited 424 times between 1999 and 2014. While I do not mean to suggest that in each citation her work is functioning to support a claim being made about the abolition of the universal requirement specifically, I do argue that this data suggests that her study remains particularly relevant to the field, especially in our current moment. In fact, between 2010 and 2013 *Composition in the University* was cited 98 times, appearing as evidence in several dissertations (e.g., Steven Holmes's "Actants, Agents, and Assemblages: Delivery and Writing in an Age of New Media"), book chapters (see Chris Carter's "Marketing Excellence in Higher Education" in Olson's and Worsham's, *Education as Civic Engagement: Toward a More*

Democratic Society), and academic books (see among many others Sidney I. Dobrin's *Postcomposition*). Furthermore, relatively recent studies like Daniel P. Coffey's "A Discipline's Composition: A Citation Analysis of Composition Studies" confirm the prevalence of Crowley's study in WorldCat holdings since it was first published. He notes that there were 352 holdings for *Composition in the University* between 1996 and 1998. On the surface this data may seem noteworthy only to students of library science, but this should in fact concern any scholar invested in the teaching of writing. Along these lines, and because the rhetorical nature of citation systems is discussed less in composition studies (since 1998 Connors's examination of citation practices has been cited only 27 times), this chapter emphasizes how citation practices inform the process of academic inquiry more generally, shaping the ways in which some in our field have come to "see Crowley."

Indeed, it appears that when issues related to rhetoric and composition more generally arise in composition scholarship, we are, in many cases, asked to "see Crowley" on any number of arguments, historical figures, and positions directly and indirectly related to the abolition of the universal requirement. As such, scholars have constructed Crowley's new abolitionist stance in such a way that her perspective and methodology have come to stand in for an entire tradition of abolitionism that stretches back to the inception of composition in the 1880s. Drawing threads from Robert Connors's work on the rhetoric of citations, specifically his research on the role of assumed knowledge in citations, I explain how particular citation practices relying on assumed bodies of knowledge have helped to elevate Crowley's position. I conclude this chapter by considering how specific references to Crowley's polemic function rhetorically to construct her position in the "tradition of complaint" as a master narrative, and in doing so, overshadow the participation of many other voices in this curious and persistent debate.

THE PARTICULARS OF A POWERFUL POLEMIC

In this section, I clarify the particulars of Crowley's polemic. Because citations to Crowley tend toward generalities about her role and the specifics of her argument, I will in this section review important subtleties of her position. In *Composition in the University: Historical and Polemical Essays*, Crowley outlines a very specific polemic. She writes:

> In this spirit, I offer a modest proposal. Let's abolish the universal requirement. Let's just stop insisting that every student who enrolls in a two-year college or four-year university must take a required composition course. Please note that I am *not* proposing the abolition of introductory-level writing courses. (242)

In this, we have the basis of her position as well as a quasi-rebuttal, one anticipating confusion or misreading. It is because she anticipates confusion that I think we have reason to delve deeper into her assertions. After all, "In this spirit" suggests that her proposal grows out of previous claims and evidence, an argument that is more complex than the issue at hand. This distinction between abolishing the universal requirement and abolishing introductory composition altogether is also important to note: it indicates that Crowley is aware of the history of the abolition debate, and she clearly believes that her audience is as well. However, even more striking is the implicit rhetorical strategy in the expression, "I offer a modest proposal" (242). The sincerity and obvious commitment to students and composition in which the entire work is grounded is a far cry from the ironic and satiric disposition of Jonathan Swift, to which "a modest proposal" presumably refers. In his review of *Composition in the University*, Raúl Sánchez notes that the irony of this subtitle cannot be overlooked, and that understanding the ways in which "Academic-ideological forces" (Crowley 229) buttress the claims of Crowley's argument might be more important than considering counter-arguments in support of compulsory composition. Crowley articulates how these forces are at play in compulsory freshman English by recounting an incident at the University of Texas at Austin in 1990.

Crowley reports that at this time the committee responsible for managing freshman English at the University of Texas at Austin designed and put into place a new syllabus, "Writing About Difference." The syllabus included several court cases, which according to Crowley, were selected for a couple of reasons:

> First, there were associated documents in each case that took a variety of positions with regard to its merit—majority and minority opinions from several courts along with law review articles; second, each case raised the issue of what it means to be defined as different from mainstream American culture. (230)

Drawing from Stephen Toulmin's "data/warrant/claim model of argumentation," students were asked to perform "traditional" writing tasks like summaries and also to write in "small and large groups" (230). What Crowley describes is a quintessential "process"-oriented approach to freshman composition pedagogy. For the early 1990s, apart from the emphasis on court cases, which were used as primary sources for this syllabus, the UT pedagogy was not groundbreaking, especially if you consider that the use of Stephen Toulmin's theoretical methodology dates back to the mid-1960s.

Nevertheless, Crowley reports that a "very public uproar followed the English Department's adoption of this proposed syllabus" (230). This discord led to the "permanent postponement" of the use of the syllabus at Texas.

Crowley asserts that on one level, criticisms of the syllabus seemed politically motivated. "Conservative critics," she writes, ". . . who included the Texas branch of the National Association of Scholars and commentator George Will, interpreted the focus on "difference" as a politically correct indoctrination in racism and sexism" (230). More interesting, though, to Crowley is the fact that faculty members outside of the UT English department and members of the press were equally disturbed by the syllabus. In Crowley's eyes, these outsiders were people "who literally had no professional or financial stake in the design of the course" and possessed little to no knowledge in the history, theory, and teaching of freshman English. These critics were outsiders in another regard; they were also unfamiliar with the growing field of composition studies. Crowley concludes that this incident demonstrates the ways we might think about freshman English as a public utility, or in her words, as cultural capital (229), "as the mutual property of all persons who conceive of education as a site for transmission of a received dominant culture" (231). She determines that the source of people's frustration with the syllabus was not as political as some might expect. Instead, she concludes that "correct" English—a commitment deep within "America's cultural imagination" (231)—was at the heart of this dispute.

American universities' discriminatory practices based on race and class are inextricably linked to the desire for "correct" and proper English, which Crowley characterizes as having a long and complex history that extends to attitudes about literacy more generally. Although Crowley broadens her analytical framework to include concerns about literacy, she eventually narrows her scope both to the idealist notions of "correct" English and also the "idealist notion of 'the academic essay' "(233). Of the five-paragraph essay she notes, "it fosters and supports the persistent American belief that universal standards of literacy exist, and it legitimizes and covers over the social and institutional functions of Freshman English" (233). The "social and institutional functions" of first-year writing are intertwined with and affected by a penchant to either embrace the myth of the academic essay or reject it, replacing it with what might be best characterized as the grand narrative of literacy and empowerment. Not surprisingly, for Crowley, both moves, in their own way, replicate the discourse—the political, social, and institutional semiotics—as well as the conditions that valorize the aforementioned idealist myths of composition. This leads to discriminatory and unfair conditions for both students and instructors and necessitates the type of change that Crowley has in mind: namely, the abolition of the universal requirement of freshman English.

CROWLEY AND THE RISE OF NEW ABOLITIONISM

In addition to accounting for some of the overlooked particulars of Crowley's proposal, another aim of this study is to examine the ways and reasons for which Crowley's call is so popular in contemporary composition studies. One way we can gain some insight into this matter is by examining how her proposal was initially received by the field of composition studies.

In his history of the abolition debate, Robert Connors notes that Crowley's polemic and her criticism of the universal requirement is so significant that it marks a critical turning point in the debate. For Connors, Crowley's study marks the beginning of what he terms the "New Abolitionist" movement, a period marked by calls for the abolition of compulsory English from the ranks of "composition insiders" (21), not literature faculty, as had been the case in the past.[1] Without a doubt, Crowley is a composition insider, as she has received considerable acclaim within the field of rhetoric and composition for her study *The Methodical Memory: Invention in Current-Tradition Rhetoric*. In addition, *Composition in the University* won the 1998 Mina Shaughnessy Prize, which is, according to the Modern Language Association, "presented for an outstanding scholarly book in the fields of language, culture, literacy, or literature with strong application to the teaching of English." Certainly, this professional status coupled with the "deliberately provocative" (Connors 21) diction and tone of her text has contributed, in part, to the notoriety of this particular proposal to abolish compulsory freshman English. However, when we turn to reviews of the work we find dramatically conflicting statements with respect to the value of the text for the field of composition and rhetoric.

In his review of Crowley's work in *The Journal of Advanced Composition*, Raúl Sánchez writes quite highly of the text. Above all he appreciates the study's methodology, which he describes as a version of "postmodern historiography." Although we get little sense of what this term explicitly means to him, what counts as history for Sánchez are the many topics that Crowley touches on in her revisionist history of freshman English: namely, the rise of Arnoldian humanism and of literary studies at the expense of composition; the privatization of the rhetorical canon of invention (which Crowley also discusses in *The Methodical Memory*); the influence of the trend toward academic specialization in universities; and, finally, pressures brought on by World War II, the General Education Movement, and responses to fascism and communism. Sánchez is right when he mentions that most in composition are familiar with aspects of this narrative, one that pits freshman English in a power struggle against these aforementioned pressures and developments. However, what is most interesting about his reception of Crowley's study is that his *only* criticism of the work is precisely what he admires most about it.

> Given that humanism has been under attack for some time now—from within both composition theory and literary theory, as Crowley notes—its role as scapegoat in this narrative will make quite good

> sense to many readers. But precisely because assent is so easily achieved on this matter—because terms like "Arnoldian humanism" are now familiar pejoratives in the lexicon of English studies—it merits more careful scrutiny than Crowley offers here and throughout the book. While she does offer a discursive footnote that addresses humanism's various definitions and applications in education, one is left, nonetheless, with the impression that a revisionist history of composition requires a similarly revisionist account of humanism, if the two are as intertwined as Crowley suggests.

Sánchez seems to value Crowley's study because it provides a historical context for the claims that she makes in earlier criticisms of compulsory freshman English. In fact, somewhat surprisingly, he notes that it is this attention to historical context (not her specific proposals or polemical tone) that drives the study. He notes, "*Composition in the University* uses history to advance its argument, to make its case—not to tell what happened, not to tell *the truth*." Sánchez feels so strongly about Crowley's methodology that he thinks the book itself should be *compulsory* for graduate students in composition and rhetoric. "Thus," he writes, "the book is an example of the kind of empirical/archival/theoretical work that is possible in composition studies, and for that reason alone it should be *required* reading in our graduate programs" (emphasis added). If Sánchez's review is an example of the type of reception that has contributed to Crowley's polemic gaining currency and credibility in the field of rhetoric and composition, then the following essay points to how divisive Crowley's work is.

Two years later, writing in *Rhetoric Society Quarterly*, Jacqueline Rhodes stops well short of recommending that Crowley's proposal be required reading for graduate students in English studies. In fact, instead of advocating a wider reception for the text, she cautions readers that Crowley's "prognosticatory" (98) essays are not for everyone. "The book is not for the faint of heart," she writes, "nor for those unwilling to question just what it is we do as rhetoricians and/or composition specialists" (98). Despite her reservations she is, like Sánchez, interested in Crowley's methodology, which she describes as a "recasting of the history of composition" (96), allowing Crowley a strategic "place from which to argue for the abolition of Freshman English" (96). Rhodes criticizes Crowley for her "loose" and "interweaving" history (which might lend some insight into what Sánchez means by "postmodern historiography"), and she notes that "the book seems to rush at the issues from all sides" (96).

In addition to these concerns about her methodology, Rhodes has reservations about Crowley's proposal to abolish the universal requirement of freshman English specifically:

> However, by the end of this cogent exploration, I was still waiting for the "what then?" of Crowley's argument. That is, if contemporary rhetoricians, compositionists, teachers, and administrators do all eventually agree on Crowley's course of action, what are the intellectual and material consequences? What happens to those rhetoricians and compositionists, the adjunct instructors, the graduate teaching assistants, and—importantly—the students themselves? (98).

It is important to note that Rhodes's misgivings should not be confused with a common trope of the genre of book reviews. Rhodes is engaged in an act of speculation, but she is not speculating about how Crowley's work will be received by the field of rhetoric and composition more generally. This is, without a doubt, a move that characterizes most reviews of scholarly publications in English studies. Instead, I argue that what we find here is a symptom of the rhetorical power and influence of Crowley's proposal to abolish compulsory freshman English. Simply put, Rhodes is frightened by the implications of Crowley's proposal. She seems legitimately concerned about what will happen if the field acts together to abolish the universal requirement, and the fact that she strings together question after rhetorical question points to how uncertain and anxious Crowley's text leaves her. In addition to worrying about the intellectual and material consequences of abolishing the universal requirement, Rhodes is also apprehensive about how the field will be perceived. She expresses her most serious concerns with one last rhetorical question: "it is not my intention," she writes, "to buttress the composition empire against which Crowley argues; rather, I wonder who it is we would be *without* that structure. What would composition offer as its public rationale?" (98).

Certainly, Rhodes's response highlights the ways that the image or public identity of the field of rhetoric and composition is linked to the universal requirement. However, for now, I want to stress that Rhodes's response is indicative of just how polarizing and divisive Crowley's proposal is. On the one hand, we have Sánchez's review, which more or less advocates the canonization of Crowley's call to abolish compulsory freshman English, despite his expressed ambivalence about her methodology. On the other hand, we find Rhodes cautioning readers, restricting the scope of the essay's reception, questioning the ends toward which Crowley's proposal is directed, and, in a sense, reacting unfavorably to its influence.

Unfortunately, what I suspect has occurred is that over time both scenarios have played out. Because *Composition in the University* is cited so frequently and in other *compulsory* studies (as we will see in the next section), the text has become required reading for graduate students in rhetoric and composition seminars and programs. Consequently, graduate students, sometimes at very early stages in their studies, experience many of the same anxieties and doubts expressed by Rhodes when they first learn that there is an undercurrent in their chosen profession that seeks to abolish the requirement for freshman English, the very topic of study to which many have committed their professional lives. This was certainly my experience when I first encountered Crowley's study as a graduate student, and after reading Rhodes's review of her work I know that I was not alone in my ambivalence, nor were my trepidations unfounded. The consequences of this situation are impossible to evaluate fully, but we can learn even more about how Crowley's study has come to stand in for the entire tradition of abolitionism and complaint by examining more closely the ways that Crowley's study functions on evidentiary levels in rhetoric and composition scholarship.

THE RHETORIC OF CITATIONS—EXPLICATING TYPOGRAPHICAL ENDS

Up to this point I have discussed the particulars of Crowley's polemic, but now I turn to a discussion of annotation and citation. More specifically, I discuss the rhetoric of citation systems. In many ways, the following discussion aims to pin down a language to discuss the function of citations in scholarly inquiry. I do not aspire, however, to give voice to *every* contributor to this lengthy and expansive line of inquiry on the nature and function of footnotes and other forms of annotation in scholarly research. I aim to lend support to a critical assumption at the heart of my argument in this study: citation systems and other references function rhetorically both because of the substantive content they contain and because of the forms in which they appear.

In this next section, I review Shirley K. Rose's discussion of citation practices in the context of metaphor, extending the discourse of economics to account for prevailing understandings of how citation systems function in writing. Robert J. Connors provides a history of citation systems and emphasizes what is implied by Rose, namely, that annotations are directly linked to social and rhetorical concerns. Finally, Kay Halasek demonstrates what is at stake in any inquiry directed toward delineating a rhetoric of citation systems. She suggests that any discussion of reported speech—in any form—presupposes rhetorical concerns to some degree.

In "The Role of Scholarly Citations in Disciplinary Economies," Rose hopes that by extending "economic metaphors" to examples of citation practices, she may provide insight into how various citation systems function to limit participation in and distribution of knowledge within communities. Rose describes how citation systems contribute to the sense of a continuity of practice in scholarship. For instance, in examining references to Mina

Shaughnessy's *Errors and Expectations*, she delineates eight types of "coherence relationships" (246) that may be evinced from examining a "grammar of citations" (244). In her sixth example, which is most applicable to my study, Rose analyzes Maxine Hairston's reference to Shaughnessy in a passage from "The Winds of Change: Thomas Kuhn and the Revolution in the Teaching of Writing":

> [Shaughnessy] was the first to undertake a large-scale research project whose goal was to teach the new students of the seventies to write. Her example, her book, and her repeated calls for new research in composition have undoubtedly been important stimuli in spurring the profession's search for a new paradigm. (Hairston qtd. in Rose 246)

Here, Rose identifies this citation (as she does with the other categories) in terms of a relationship between the text cited and the text in which the citation appears. For Rose, this type of citation suggests a "sequential relationship"—or a chronological ordering of texts—one that is "especially significant" (246). Rose stops shorts of articulating precisely why this relationship is so significant, though she does state, "Ordering texts chronologically makes very specific claims about their significance to the orderly development of a discipline" (246). Certainly, Rose's fine study yields significant insights, but she also confirms what many teacher-researchers already know about footnotes: because citations often contain names, titles—and of course, *dates*—they contribute to a sense of temporal continuity in scholarship, thereby providing a sense that research constitutes various positions in a narrative directed toward certain ends. In other words, footnotes often function to order scholarly and deliberative inquiry—to situate research and scholars on a timeline.

Robert Connors's study of citation systems interrogates footnotes and other forms of annotation from a perspective highly sensitive to time. In addition, he demonstrates that when discussing the nature of citation styles, we find ourselves deep in matters of rhetoric. In part I, "The Development of Annotation Structures from the Renaissance to 1900" Connors presents an intriguing historical overview of the development of citations in Western culture. However, behind his attempt to recount this curious history is another project (certainly one just as curious): to foreground his study of citation in rhetorical matters. As he begins his study he notes,

> The field of rhetoric, especially in its written forms, where citations had to be visible and reproducible, inevitably evolved the most formalized conventions for signaling ethical use of others'

> work. The gradual formalization of written citation systems should not, however, blind us to their essentially rhetorical nature. Every formal structure declares allegiances and counterallegiances. (338)

Indeed, for Connors, the act of reporting others' work—of footnoting, annotating, and citing—*begins* with rhetoric. That is, the essences of persuasion—*logos*, *ethos*, *pathos*, and *kairos*—already inform the formal structure of citations. Consequently, rhetoric and ethics underline citation systems and structures even before they are deployed. As Ede and Lunsford note in the preface to part I of "The Rhetoric of Citation Systems," the title of Connors's article ends with an asterisk that points readers to Connors's own rather lengthy footnote, one that fully demonstrates the essential rhetorical nature of citation systems (338). Connor states:

> Readers will notice that this essay violates *Rhetoric Review's* own citation style, which follows New MLA in asking for endnotes rather than footnotes. I specifically requested this change of the editor, and she has graciously assented. . . . I have simply found footnotes a more precise system, allowing for a text/note dialogism that endnotes kill completely. And given the fact that the only footnotes still allowed by New MLA are discursive, that dialogism is even more important. (337)

Here, Connors demonstrates that a violation of an audience's or an editorial staff's expectations of citation formats requires a rationale—the requisite conditions of rebuttal. Simply put, his citation style demonstrates the "inescapably social" (338) and rhetorical nature of annotations more generally.

Still, a significant part of the rhetorical nature of citation systems involves the extent to which annotations and references rely on, among other things, assumptions about what knowledge readers possess. By this I mean that, at times, the effectiveness of citations partly depends on whether readers are familiar with content referenced in the citation. For instance, as Connors details in his discussion of the 1582 Rheims New Testament, which used a system of "endnotes glosses" (351) after each chapter, this version of the New Testament assumed a great deal about its audience—and for good reason:

> The work assumes familiarity with a body of commenting literature; it uses specialized Latinate "insider" terminology to direct readers around within its field of interlocking claims and support; it uses these citations to support specific textual positions recognizable within a discourse community; and it backs its positions by careful

> reference to accredited masters working previously within that community. (351)

Connors's assessment is all the more remarkable because it is in reference to what he deems an "overtly polemical" work. As Connors remarks on the role of citation formats during this time, the "glossings" and references present in the Rheims New Testament were, in part, a response to a dispute over annotation styles specifically. In the sixteenth century, the Geneva Bible of 1560 and the Bishops' Bible of 1568—both Protestant publications—demonstrated the extent to which typographical methods had advanced, as each used "textual letter citations—a, b, c, d—to refer to glosses printed in small type in the margins and at the foot of the page" (351). Such sophisticated citation methods allowed for filling of the vast white space surrounding blocks of text with marginal comments and specific translation or explanation remarks. Most importantly, however, these citation systems were couched in "typological precedents," standards that virtually guaranteed a consistent and "coherent Protestant reading" (351). Not surprisingly, and as Connors explains in his study, the Catholics had an innovative response of their own: the Rheims New Testament. In contrast to the Geneva Bible and the Bishops' Bible, the presence of endnotes (rather than simply marginal or interlinear annotation) guaranteed, as one might expect, a biblical reading in opposition to the type of "coherence" emphasized by Protestant versions. In fact, the Rhemish form of citation aspired not to achieve a state of coherence but "to minimize the *rhetorical* effect of extensive notational apparatus" (351). What is most interesting, I think, is that contrary to what we might expect, it is not the momentous task of translation or quarrels over doctrinal paradigms that motivated new versions of the Bible during this time. Instead, it was a dispute over annotation styles. More specifically, the rhetorical potential implicit in these citation styles galvanized participants of this debate.

Beyond such disputes, the Rheims New Testament introduced other citation styles that, according to Connors, "would ever after exist" (351): the *dialogic* note and the *citation* note. The dialogic or discursive note literally undergirds the main text, providing related commentary for the purpose of establishing relationships between elements in the text. The citation note, on the other hand, communicates precise information to provide access to a particular text quoted by an author. Not unexpectedly, and as I argue, it is precisely when we begin drawing distinctions within citation systems that we find ourselves very much in matters of rhetoric. This is, I think, because the distinctions we draw often reveal the ends we aspire to achieve. And in many ways, Kay Halasek demonstrates how social, cultural, and political underpinnings specifically inform these aspirations and our annotations as well.

Throughout *A Pedagogy of Possibility*, Halasek provides readers with a theory of composition pedagogy that privileges dialogic explanations of learning over monologic ones—dynamic conceptions of students' relationship to discourse rather than static ones. She foregrounds this theoretical paradigm—as well as a reconceived notion of writing instruction—in principles of heteroglossia and dialogue, concepts that serve as cornerstones of Bakhtinian language theory. A critical facet of her thesis is most clear in a discussion of the forms and significance of reported speech; however, her position on the "politics" of citation systems differs slightly from that of Robert Connors and, to some extent, Shirley Rose.

In Halasek's analysis of representations of "summary and paraphrase" in composition textbooks, she takes issue, as Connors and Rose might, with the notion that "summary and paraphrase alone *and not direct or indirect* quotation are capable of reporting another's discourse in a critical manner" (162). Such an argument, she asserts, overlooks the dialogic relationship reported discourse shares with the main text of a written composition. More strikingly, however, near the end of this discussion she argues that "it's not the *form* that the reporting discourse takes that determines its orientation toward the reported discourse but the *style* of that reporting discourse" (163). This assertion, in part, contradicts the assumption that is at the heart of Connors' and Rose's claims about the rhetoricity of citation systems, that the descriptive category of a citation—its *form* alone—presupposes rhetorical matters. As we have seen with other authors' attempts to make sense of the rhetorical underpinnings of reported speech, Halasek offers a new articulation to distinguish between types of citations. Nevertheless, it is this tendency, I think—to name, locate, and distinguish—that articulates the stakes in this discussion of the rhetoric of citation systems, and in my identification and analysis of the rhetorical purpose of scholars' injunctions to "see Crowley."

SEE THE MATERIAL CONDITIONS OF COMPOSITION INSTRUCTORS

The epigraph from Kay Halasek which begins this chapter touches on the degree to which rhetorical concerns and consequences permeate discussions of reported speech. Here I am interested in considering the rhetorical consequences of referencing Crowley's polemic in the context of materialist critiques of composition studies. However, I am also interested in the degree to which citations rely on assumptions about the knowledge readers possess to realize these rhetorical consequences. The scholars I treat in the following section all refer to Crowley's polemic in various ways. Delineating these different ways and the tendencies implicit in each citation serves to improve how we report the speech of others in composition scholarship and our understanding of how Crowley's call has come to eclipse an entire tradition of complaint.

First, we turn to Joseph Harris's "Meet the New Boss, Same as the Old Boss: Class Consciousness in Composition." In this study, Harris's chief concern is to call attention to conflicts of interest brought on by the varying and unethical material conditions under which many composition instructors work. More specifically, however, he is concerned with how the field of rhetoric and composition discusses this issue. He demonstrates that when questions explicitly concerned with the material conditions of composition instruction arise, various members of the field (not only part-timers and graduate assistants, but also tenure-track faculty and administrators) often elide matters involving class consciousness by situating such discussions in terms of "professional and disciplinary" (46) contexts. Although Harris seems captivated by the idea that conflicts of interest pertaining to departmental roles lead to misguided perceptions of the value of work, he is in fact less concerned with the disciplinary status of composition than he is with improving the material conditions of instruction for composition and the quality of that instruction for undergraduates. He explains:

> But while I, too, am concerned with how scholarly work in composition gets valued (or not), the crucial questions for me are still these: Who does the actual teaching? What institutional structures best allow us to shape how writing gets taught to undergraduates? I am less worried, that is, about the status of composition as a discipline than about whether composition programs treat instructors fairly and teach undergraduates to write well. (56)

He suggests that teacher-researchers in composition have "succumbed to a professional logic" (56), which holds that if composition studies is considered a "research field," the teaching of writing will improve. Of course, the claims of this logic are bolstered by many assumptions, some of which Harris details: most notably, this logic assumes that tenured faculty constitute all research fields and that opening more lines of tenure in composition studies improves the quality of writing instruction and the intellectual merit or status of the discipline. Ultimately, Harris crunches the numbers of this quandary and concludes, "But there will never be close to enough tenure-stream compositionists to teach all the sections of first-year writing offered at US colleges and universities each year . . ." (56). It is with this deconstruction of a particularly tenacious theme in composition scholarship that Harris proceeds to his own discussion of the abolition debate—a discussion that is directly linked with his suggestions for improving the material conditions of composition instruction.

In Harris's discussion of the debate over compulsory composition, as in his discussion of the materiality of composition programs more generally, he situates the debate as part of a depth of inquiry, one with its own narrative, history, antagonists, and—dare I say—heroes. His seventh footnote reads:

> See Crowley's *Composition in the University* and also the essays in Joseph Petraglia's *Reconceiving Writing, Rethinking Writing Instruction*. For a powerful counter to the "New Abolitionism," see Roemer, Schultz, and Durst's recent essay on "Reframing the Great Debate on First-Year Writing." (66)

This footnote is particularly revelatory for my study: it is a glancing reference to a complex debate, one that is defined by assumptions about the purpose, viability, and future of writing in universities. On the surface, Harris's footnote functions to bolster his claims, insofar as it appropriately acknowledges principal contributors to the abolition debate. However, it also relies on an assumed body of knowledge. I mean that for readers to navigate the debate—and arguably, recognize the significance of this footnote—they must have, at the very least, a sense of what part of *Composition in the University* Harris specifically refers to; an idea as to what extent Petraglia's selected essays comment on what Harris finds so salient in Crowley's proposal; how "New Abolitionism" differs from the original version of abolitionism; and finally, knowledge as to what characteristics—in composition scholarship specifically—constitute "powerful" responses.

It is striking, in my opinion, how Connors's assertions on the function of citations in the Rheims New Testament account for what is happening in Harris's citation of Crowley. As I mentioned earlier, Connors states that many citations in the 1582 Rheims New Testament—like Harris's—*assume* familiarity with a body of commenting literature, rely on "insider" language or jargon to "direct readers around within its field of interlocking claims and support," and deploy citations to bolster "positions recognizable within a discourse community" (351). Most notable and revealing in the context of this study, however, is Connors's last point: citations in the Rheims New Testament back recognizable positions by referencing the previous work of "accredited masters" in a particular discourse community. I think it is safe to assert that Crowley is an "accredited master" in composition studies. Although this might be an unsettling position for her to hold, she might agree with the assertion that citations that reference her work as Harris does partly construct her position as a master narrative within the abolition debate. But as I have demonstrated, this privileged and valorized position comes at the cost of not fully representing critical facets of her argument—in a sense, silencing Crowley in a reference intended to give her a voice.

The question, then, becomes: to what extent do the inherent assumptions in Harris's footnote allow him to achieve a particular rhetorical purpose in his study? Earlier I remarked that Harris explicitly states that he is less interested in interrogating the status of composition than he is in offering an alternative to this established line of inquiry. What I think is most interesting about this qualifying language is that while Harris argues that the category of status is not a principal concern of his text, he raises the issue implicitly simply by referencing Crowley's position in the abolition debate. However, as Connors shows us, it is possible that the argument over the status of composition is *understood* in Harris's reference to Crowley. Like the understood "you" in the language of Harris's citation ([You] see Crowley) or the assumed body of knowledge at play in citations in the Rheims New Testament, her unique historical methodology and discussion of the relegation of composition studies are understood in Harris's citation. It seems that while concerns over the status of composition are not a principal orientation for Harris, they are important undercurrents at the most critical moment in his study. After all, it is in Harris's conclusion that he makes specific recommendations for improving the material conditions of composition studies.

Harris's citation of Crowley suggests some of the consequences that stem from relying on an assumed body of knowledge in citations, concerns outlined and remarked on by Connors. Similarly, we can look at Bruce Horner's reference of Crowley and see the importance of sequence and the significance of the relationships that comprise such sequences, ideas expressed by Shirley Rose. In *Terms of Work for Composition: A Materialist Critique*, Horner, like Harris, argues that many scholars in composition studies turn a blind eye to the social and material conditions that underlie the daily operations of their work. Much of his text deals with how teacher-researchers construct student identities and roles based on perceived intellectual and performative potential. Such moves, according to Horner, can serve to elide the fact that more than anything, students often signal the significance and presence of the materiality of our work in composition. To this end, then, Horner marshals an understanding of the "political" as "an inescapable dimension of all human life" (74) rather than as a condition of the intentionally naïve. In this vein, "Academic," the fourth chapter of Horner's study, continues his examination of the functioning of contradictions in academic representations of work. Here, Horner's study begins to take its intended shape as an exploration into why teacher-researchers perceive divisions among academic, professional, and political discourses, and how specific interpretive moves serve to replicate consequences of conceptualizing such differences. This is most clear, I believe, in Horner's treatment of the abolition debate in composition studies. Quoting from Crowley's "The Perilous Life and Times of Freshman English," Horner writes:

> Sharon Crowley, for example, argues that the "heart" of the problems of "Freshman English" arises from its "unusual origin" "as a response to perceived deficiencies in students' literate skills, rather than as an arena in which to study a body of received knowledge." Thus, "the course has never appropriated an area of study for itself that would bring order to its teaching" (126).

Horner's reference to Crowley differs from Rose's example (using Shaughnessy) in the sense that it does not explicitly demonstrate a sequential relationship. His reference does, however, more fully point to the significance of how we perceive the origins and outcome of the abolition debate—the significance of what Rose calls "sequential relationships." Here, Horner is setting up for an important distinction that provides two implicit orientations that, I argue, drive the rest of his study. Horner distinguishes between *functionalist* and *situated* explanations.

Functionalist explanations confuse effects with function—outcomes with origin. Conversely, situated explanations, insofar as they somewhat paradoxically aspire to make sense of functions, account for the contingency-laden underpinnings of institutions and communities. That is to say, situated explanations allow for complexity and the possibility that institutions sometimes perform functions that seemingly contradict their intended purpose. As such, we can better understand the rhetorical consequences of situated references by turning to what Horner finds so problematic about Crowley's role in the abolition debate. He writes:

> The same confusion obtains in debates over the abolition of freshman composition. The arguments for abolishing freshman composition typically attribute to the course the performance of some function, whether praised or condemned, in relation either to non-academic social needs or other academic work. (126)

For Horner, a fundamental flaw of the abolition argument is that it presumes that the origin narrative of the institutional form "inevitably functions to realize that potential" (133). That is, because the abolition argument partly depends on Crowley's conception of a "unique origin" narrative, *functionalist* explanations tend to assume that the same reasons for that narrative inform the actual work of composition today. As Horner notes, Charles Bazerman articulates a significant dilemma at the heart of this mode of thinking: "Just because we have been funded with a reductionist notion of our task has not meant that we have been bound to follow through in a reductionist way" (qtd. in Horner 130). By advancing an "authoritative" origin narrative for composition studies, we blind ourselves "to aspects and effects of such forms outside the ken of such 'norms'" (130).

Horner's reference to Crowley is important, then, because it allows him to articulate a significant consequence of advancing an "authoritative" origin narrative or a hero that is not necessarily so. Taken together, Rose and Connors suggest that, on the one hand, references that assume sequential relationships establish a sense of continuity and linearity that may not actually exist. On the other hand, taken in the context of Horner's larger project, his reference to Crowley allows him to marshal a way of thinking that accounts for a dialectical and more situated explanation of composition's unique history. This is relevant for our discussion here because, as Horner demonstrates, Crowley's polemic grows out of *her* understanding of composition's unique history. Horner demonstrates that a situated explanation of the abolition debate seems less likely to replicate reductive interpretive moves that confuse the origin of composition with its contemporary aspirations and needs. In this case, Horner's reference to Crowley does not rely on assumed knowledge, resists the tendency to valorize Crowley's position in the abolition debate, and accounts for significant particulars of her position. As such it demonstrates how the style and format of Horner's citation to Crowley's polemic is as important as the ends toward which his discussion of her text is directed.

If Horner's reference to Crowley demonstrates the significance of better situating Crowley's role in the abolition debate, then a final reference most fully models what Lisa Ede describes as a *situated* reference. In the following section, I introduce Ede's citations of Crowley as a final example, returning to Halasek in order to provide a perspective from which to discuss the significance of Ede's reference to Crowley.

(RE) SITUATING SHARON CROWLEY'S POLEMIC

In *Situating Composition: Composition Studies and the Politics of Location*, Lisa Ede details many of the assumptions that are at play in composition studies. She dovetails historical and theoretical critiques with personal experience to provide productive re-readings of chief contributions to the scholarship of composition studies. Not surprisingly, in her attempts to delineate consequences of particular assumptions for the professionalization of the discipline, she discusses the debate over the universal required first-year writing course:

> Indeed, in *Composition in the University*, Crowley argues that "[t]he traditional function of the required first-year course is increasingly hard to reconcile with the professionalization and specialization that now characterize the American academy" (10). This limitation is hardly the primary reason why Crowley calls for abandoning the required first-year writing requirement. Crowley is much more concerned with the failure of the writing process movement to constitute itself as "a truly paradigmatic alternative to current-traditionalism" (212) and with the "disciplining function" (10) that the first-year requirement exerts on students. (Ede 108).

In this passage, Ede directly quotes and accounts for some of the reasons that sustain Crowley's position on the elimination of the universal first-year requirement. Yet, Ede suggests that even a direct citation from *Composition in the University* does not fully represent the complexity and dimension of this issue. She notes that the "limitation" identified is "hardly the primary reason" motivating Crowley's polemic. Interestingly, it is the limitation identified by Horner's study—the seemingly irreconcilable consequences that grow out of the disconnect between origin narratives and contemporary purposes of modern composition—that Ede finds to be insufficient. More striking, however, is that while Ede seems to anticipate some of Horner's concerns, she emphasizes something completely different from both Harris and Horner as an exigency for Crowley's *Composition in the University*: the apparent failure of the writing process movement to take hold in composition theory and application (136–137).

Kay Halasek provides a language to discuss the rhetorical purpose and significance of Ede's reference to Crowley. Her chapter, "The Politics of Reported Speech and the Ideology of Form," draws many distinctions between the varied ways that writers report the speech of others. Most applicable to this study, however, is the distinction Halasek draws between linear and pictorial styles. Drawing on Valentin Volosinov's *Marxism and the Philosophy of Language*, Halasek suggests that linear and pictorial styles are each, in their own way, symptomatic of varied aspirations—conscious and unconscious signals that reveal more about how environments construct writers than the particular characteristics that surface in an individual's composition. Halasek explains that "Linear styles of reporting discourse" are "centripetal, conservative, and present dialogue *in absentia*, with heteroglossia as a dialogizing backdrop absent from the actual text" (166). Conversely, rather than aspiring to maintain the "original intention of the reported discourse" (166)—as linear styles do—pictorial styles of reported discourse, "incorporate heteroglossia—with its clashing and mixing of alien languages—directly into the utterance" (166). In other words, pictorial discourse (which Halasek also terms as *ludic*) provides the opportunity for readers "to question, interrogate, or even dismiss the reported discourse" (167).

I want to emphasize that I am not drawing on Halasek to suggest that the categories she delineates apply perfectly to the reported speech of Harris, Horner, or Ede. In fact, I would argue that Halasek's definition of linear discourse might be revised to account not only for the desire to preserve the "original" authorial intention of a work but also the *implied* intention. As such, it becomes quite difficult to argue that any reported discourse falls completely under the theoretical framework of either the linear or ludic style. Nevertheless, Halasek's distinction allows us to uncover both similarities and differences in reported speech, both of which—as I speculated earlier—point to the rhetorical purpose and significance of citation forms. For this reason, we might read Ede's reference to Crowley as both linear and ludic. Doing so, I think, brings us closer to a situated understanding of how Crowley functions in Ede's reference and perhaps why Ede's style of annotation leaves readers with more to work with—more opportunities for productive and generative deliberation on the abolition debate itself.

Although direct quotations from Crowley constitute much of Ede's reference, Connors would likely describe Ede's reference as "allowing for a text/note dialogism" (337) that an endnote and even a footnote does not allow. The fact that the reference to Crowley is intertextual maximizes the rhetorical effect of the citation and minimizes the disruption that footnotes would create. We see little in the way of maintaining what Rose terms as a "sequential relationship"; however, by reading the citation from both the linear and the ludic orientations, we do uncover what Rose might deem to be "especially significant" (246). If we assume that linear citation forms preserve authorial intention, then the most obvious symptom of the linear form in this reference is that Ede strings together two direct quotations from Crowley rather than, say, paraphrasing. Furthermore, in keeping with Halasek's definition of linear citations, the structure or citation form betrays the rhetorical purpose of the reference. By that, I mean, the point of Ede's citation—to both reference Crowley's role in the abolition debate and provide an alternative to generally conceded motivations for her role in that debate—is, in part, undermined by the citation form, which Halasek calls centripetal. This form obfuscates dialogue by presenting artificial resolutions and associations. Doing so, as I argue, presents and preserves what the writer—in this case, Ede—determines to be the authorial intention—the *perceived* intention of Crowley.

Conversely, in order to read Ede's citation as pictorial or ludic, we must uncover the tendency to retort and parody reported speech, a centrifugal quality that leads to the smearing of the boundaries "between authorial, or reporting, and reported discourse through commentary and evaluation"

(Halasek 166). We do not find examples of parody in Ede's reference to Crowley; however, we do find language that indicates a sort of stepping out, an analytical and evaluative move that lends perspective on Crowley's scholarly influence. For instance, Ede notes, "This limitation is hardly the primary reason why Crowley calls for abandoning the required first-year writing requirement" (108). Here, in essence, we find Ede speaking for Crowley. When she writes, "This limitation is hardly" she seems to suggest that what is to follow has been overlooked; moreover, that this point is not buried in an endnote, or setting below a horizon of inquiry at the bottom of the page, indicates the level of importance of this matter for Ede; she is maximizing the rhetorical effect of this reference by accounting for a commonly overlooked reason of Crowley's polemic. In so doing, I believe Ede effectively models a situated reference to Crowley's study. She provides readers with a reference to the abolition debate that attempts to account for one of the most cited but least understood voices in the debate: Crowley's. As Halasek writes,

> The measure of an effective discourse, then, is neither in the level of its originality nor in the extent to which it says something new, but rather in the extent to which it recognizes, entertains, manages, and contends with those "off-stage voices," the extent to which it effectively reports others' discourses in a ludic style. (170).

In this passage, Halasek articulates important characteristics that situated references might reflect. Interestingly, however, it is by reading Ede's reference as both linear and ludic that we come to see what is at stake in this discussion more generally.

Although the power and notoriety of Crowley's call for the abolition of the first-year requirement beckons researchers to valorize her, it may also encourage scholars to generalize about her role and influence in this debate. By this, I mean that contemporary composition scholarship tends to employ Crowley in ways that cause her to stand in for what Leonard Greenbaum calls a "tradition of complaint," one that, as I have noted, reaches back to the early 1880s and is constituted by many voices, each responding to specific pressures and times. Generalizations like these, as well as the formal structure of references and the tendencies that grow out of these citations, erase Crowley from her own polemic, in a sense silencing her in citations intended to give her voice. Scholars in composition studies would do well to examine more closely the reasons and rhetorical consequences of references to Crowley's call for the abolition of the universal first-year composition requirement. By allowing Crowley's proposal to stand in for an entire tradition of abolitionism and reform, we may indeed valorize Crowley's role in this debate, but we elide the particulars and nuance of her position and other important voices in the Great Debate.

FIVE

"WHAT SHOULD COLLEGES TEACH?"

A Proposal for a Compulsory Curriculum in First-Year Literacy Studies

Learning literacy, and whatever lies beyond it, is *hard work.*

—Harvey J. Graff, *The Labyrinths of Literacy*

The debate over composition's place in the university continues today, and with it, the questions, continuities, and myths of literacy that have perpetuated the argument since the inception of the compulsory course over a century ago. For instance, in 2009, Stanley Fish published a three-part article in the *New York Times* titled "What Should Colleges Teach?" The most striking feature of this essay is the extent to which Fish echoes the sentiments of more than a century of complaints about composition. Like Lounsbury's study in 1911 and Campbell's polemic in 1939, Fish begins his article by lamenting the declining writing and reading skills of his students. This realization lead him to perform an investigation in which he "asked to see the lesson plans of the 104 sections" of composition at a university (Fish). What Fish found confirmed his suspicions: "Although the other 100 sections fulfilled the composition requirement, instruction in composition was not their focus. Instead, the students spent much of their time discussing novels, movies, TV shows and essays on a variety of hot-button issues—racism, sexism, immigration, globalization." Fish's review of syllabi (not "lesson plans" as he previously noted) leads him to conclude that courses that do not focus on "writing" specifically are a "sham." Like Brower and Rice in the 1940s, he divides the blame between high schools and universities, noting, "I cannot see, however, why a failure of secondary education relieves college teachers of a responsibility to make up the deficit. Quite the reverse. It is because our students come to us unable to write clean English sentences that we are obligated to supply what they did not receive from their previous teachers." The blame that Fish places with both high schools and post-secondary composition instructors is certainly reminiscent of arguments and complaints about composition that have come before him. However, Fish's cursory and injudicious methodology represents an even more significant continuity in the Great Debate, especially when he remarks on what is at stake in composition, specifically, how the writing of students is invariably indicative of cognitive aptitude and quality of thinking.

From Fish's perspective, an important part of understanding the role of composition in developing and representing cognitive skills is realizing that the "content" that students write about is less important than learning the "forms" of composition. "Writing is its own subject," he writes, "and a deeper and more fascinating one than the content it makes available. Content just sprawls around; forms constrain and shape it." To support his position, he does not draw from the findings of his investigation of lesson plans, nor from research in the teaching of writing; instead, he makes use of comments left by readers online. He asserts: "As Jamakaya says, 'good writing skills instill good thinking,' not the other way around. Robin T. agrees: 'Young people who can't write can't think.'" On the one hand, Fish's article—and the evidence he marshals—represents a unique moment in the debate, in that the participation of his readership (in the form of comments left online) become an increasingly important part of his argument as it develops over its three parts. However, it also demonstrates how invested his readership is in the debate over the aims and effectiveness of composition (the second part of his article alone received in excess of 450 comments). What we find luring both readers and Fish into the debate are exaggerated expectations about the consequences of possessing a particular type of literacy, as well as the unreasonable expectations of composition to consistently deliver these qualities and characteristics in students. Both Stanley Fish (and the commentators he uses to support his position) depend on what Brian Street, Ruth Finnegan, and others from the New Literacy Studies call strong theories of literacy. As I show throughout this book, these theories inaccurately presume that "good" writing alone is indicative of sophisticated and complex processes of thought. The irony of Fish's position is that one of his chief aims is to criticize contemporary approaches to composition for emphasizing content at the expense of instruction in form. Yet, because Fish himself is unaware of the role of myths of literacy and strong theories of literacy in his own formulation of composition, he does not realize that his pedagogical approach has its own content: namely, instructing students in the literacy myth itself.

To be fair, Fish's op-ed piece merely scratches the surface of larger issues discussed in his book-length scholarship. Writing in *Save the World on Your Own Time*, Fish's ire extends beyond concerns about writing pedagogy to questions about the more general function of higher education in our current moment. According to Fish, misguided faculty, confused administrators, and hyperbolic university mission statements are among the causes of a university system gone awry. Fish questions specifically the wisdom of course designs and scholarship taking up what he calls "larger issues," or work aimed toward ethical action in the world. In his view, universities should restrict their missions to two purposes: "(1) introduce students to bodies of knowledge and traditions of inquiry that had not previously been part of their experience; and (2) equip those same students with the analytical skills . . . that will enable them to move confidently within those traditions and to engage in independent research after a course is over" (ch. 1). Fish's concluding remarks shed light on what he really means by this when he notes that faculty should simply do their jobs (provide students with a set of skills) and "look for no pleasures beyond the pleasure of responsible, rigorous performance" (ch. 7).

Although the scope of inquiry differs in Fish's book-length study and his op-ed essay, the essence of both arguments remains the same. Both his critique of writing pedagogy and higher education rely on a skills-based conception of learning and literacy. David Barton reminds us, the "idea of skills is a particular way of thinking about literacy; it is a metaphor no less than the disease metaphor" (12). As such, Fish overlooks the more significant problem of how thinking about one thing (literacy) in terms of another thing (skills) makes possible the very approach to pedagogy that he seeks to eradicate. If—in our current technological and cultural moment—we do as Fish suggests, and restrict curricula to skills-based conceptions of learning, we should not be surprised when faculty go beyond narrow, anachronistic, and ambiguously defined learning objectives by asking students to engage in ethical action in the real world (e.g., service learning programs). Characterizing the work of universities, especially with respect to literacy, merely in terms of skills to be delivered to students, does not accurately or effectively anticipate the varied, uneven, and complex expertise that contemporary students enact in universities every day. Furthermore, and to put it bluntly, just as skills-based conceptions of engagement and learning limited Manchester's and Thurber's views of what was pedagogically possible for students in the early 1900s, so do they restrict Fish's view of what is possible for students, faculty, and universities today.

That said, I do not take up Fish in the conclusion of this project to discredit entirely his critique and proposal for reforming the teaching of writing. To be fair, I believe he rightly questions the relevance of some "orthodoxies that have taken hold in the composition world." For instance, he is particularly dubious of the 1974 Conference on College Composition and Communication (CCCC) statement that affirms students' "rights" "to their own patterns and varieties of language—the dialects of their nurture or whatever dialects in which they find their own identity and style" (CCCC).[1] However, in questioning the CCCC committee's use of the word "right" to discuss literacy instruction in composition, Fish unintentionally underscores the importance of challenging and critiquing the language we use to talk about composition and literacy more generally. After all, one danger in characterizing literacy as a "right" is that it throws into relief many of the other fundamental rights we, as a society, are unable to provide, e.g., the right to shelter, food, and clean drinking water.

Characterizing literacy as a right also positions it as an independent variable in culture, setting the stage for the abstractions, vague definitions, and assumptions that allow literacy myths to maintain such a strong hold on post-secondary English instruction. In the context of the debate over the aims, institutional significance, and effectiveness of composition, presuming that the benefits and consequences of literacy acquisition are directly related to the rights that students possess exaggerates the expectations that we have for both literacy and the institutions that provide instruction in it.

I wish to raise the possibility that there may not be any viable positions to take in the Great Debate if the terms and issues that have constrained and perpetuated the discussion for over a century are not questioned and complicated. If myths of literacy are not dealt with directly, that is, if they are not identified, complicated, and situated historically and comparatively, we can only expect more failed proposals for abolition and reform. As my study demonstrates, whether scholars are proposing that composition be reformed or abolished, the "Tradition of Complaint" seems sustained by a lack of understanding of the role of literacy myths in composition. Lamentably, because of this lack of understanding, many proposals for reform that are based on these myths unknowingly function to create the conditions that make reform necessary, causing scholars to "pursue problems with mismatched solutions," spend their energy needlessly, and accumulate despair (Cuban, "Reforming" 11).

One way out of this stale and unproductive cycle is to develop approaches to composition instruction aimed toward interrogating the very idea of literacy itself. What I envision is something very much like what composition has been engaged in for the past forty or fifty years with respect to definitions, attitudes, and understandings of the term, "rhetoric." As a discipline, composition has worked actively and enthusiastically to challenge pejorative attitudes and characterizations of rhetoric. We have explored at length the history of rhetoric and made significant steps toward appropriating the most relevant aspects of this history in order to apply them in the composition classroom. Literacy, specifically precepts and lessons of the New Literacy Studies, deserve renewed attention from the composition and rhetoric community, especially since our field is in the midst of an intellectual and pedagogical shift toward developing learning outcomes and methods of assessment around digital forms of composing.

In a March 2009 "Writer's Talk" interview with Doug Dangler, Harvey J. Graff notes that, "despite the proliferation of many proclaimed literacies today we really know surprisingly little about how they relate to each other." Graff asserts that digital literacy is "at once undersold and oversold." It is undersold in the sense that we know little about the fundamental nature of digital forms of composing, but at the same time, we sometimes seem quick to make grandiose claims, overselling significant differences between new media and textual or alphabetic literacies. One disadvantage of doing so is that we might be missing the opportunity to understand what multimodal forms of composing and print-privileged literacies have in common—what they may be able to teach each other. In my view, our current pedagogical and cultural moment provides an opportunity for first-year writing to become a site for both students and instructors to explore how multimodal and alphabetic forms of composing relate to each other.

Myths of literacy rely on grand dichotomies, perceived differences between cultures and people that possess literacy, and other unproductive (and often ethnocentric) distinctions about cognitive enhancement and social affluence. Questioning our tendency to overstate differences and distinctions among alphabetic and multimodal forms of composing is a critical step toward complicating the persistent influence of the literacy myth and strong theories of literacy on composition and English studies. Inquiry and pedagogy aimed toward identifying similarities among these various forms of composing will foster conversations and research that demand new perspectives. It is not just identifying similarities across various modes of communication that is at stake, but also finding a way to articulate the relevance of composition to universities, instructors, students, and the communities that sponsor its development in a fashion that disentangles it from the literacy myth. But making more legible the critical role of attitudes and characterizations of literacy in our relations with those interested in composition—students, administrators, policymakers, and the general public—raises difficult questions:

- If composition instruction is disentangled from the abiding belief in literacy alone to provide cognitive enhancement as well as social and economic advancement, how then does composition articulate its relevance to its institutional sponsors and critics?

- In what ways might developing curricula that emphasize understanding literacy in its specific historical, social, political, and economic contexts provide opportunities to challenge the field's persistent obsession with mechanical correctness and grammar in more effective ways?
- How might redeveloping learning outcomes and methods of assessment to engage with various forms of communication allow compositionists to teach students to question the centrality of literacy in their everyday lives?

Given how invested stakeholders in higher education are in myths of literacy, some might argue that it is unrealistic—even impossible—to expect writing programs to formulate approaches to composition instruction around such questions. However, my view is that questions like these may function as compelling points of departure for constructing learning outcomes for writing programs that take seriously the project of contesting the myths and attitudes about literacy that have sustained complaints against composition since its inception.

To be sure, other studies in the field of composition have raised related questions and proposed reforms along similar lines. Most notably, David Russell's oft-cited "Activity Theory and Its Implications for Writing Instruction" calls on the field to "raise the awareness of students, teachers, and the public *about* writing, its uses and its power—for good or ill—in the cultures and activity systems that employ it" (73). Russell asserts that the chief aim of this curriculum would be to teach students the relevance of learning about writing, rhetoric, and language, rather than learning to be better writers of a universal academic discourse that does not exist. One consequence of introducing students to these practices, according to Russell, would be that students would come away from composition with more sophisticated attitudes about writing. That is, in shifting the content of composition to the conventions and activities that constitute writing in rhetoric and language studies, the myths of "universal educated discourse" (66) and autonomous literacy would fall away from the curriculum, freeing up instructors to "teach first-year students about writing without claiming to teach students to write in general" (75). What I find so instructive and promising about Russell's argument is that questioning myths of literacy seems an implicit aim of his refiguring of composition. Although he does not connect his understanding of the myths of "universal educated discourse" and autonomous literacy to ongoing discussions of these concepts in the New Literacy Studies or to

Harvey J. Graff's work on the literacy myth, "Activity Theory and Writing Instruction" holds important lessons for writing programs interested in implementing approaches to composition aimed toward questioning myths of literacy and other tropes that have sustained criticisms of composition for over a century now.

In a similar fashion, Douglas Downs's and Elizabeth Wardle's now seminal study, "Teaching about Writing, Righting Misconceptions: (Re) Envisioning 'First-Year Composition' as 'Introduction to Writing Studies,'" proposes persuasive solutions to many of the problems I address throughout *The Lure of Literacy*. In what I believe should be compulsory reading for all teachers of composition, the authors argue that English studies must reject the idea that first-year writing can provide students with "universal academic discourse." They challenge the field to "put its money where its mouth is" by refiguring the mission of composition classes, "the very course where misconceptions" about writing are created or become even more entrenched (553). For Downs and Wardle, a course about "writing studies" asks students to explore the perennial questions related to reading and writing: "How does writing work? How do people use writing? What are the problems related to writing and reading and how can they be solved?" (558). However, instead of exploring these questions from prevailing and commonsensical perspectives, which presume that "writing is a basic, universal skill" (553) and that it can be taught by anyone, Downs and Wardle promote a pedagogy that challenges outsider's views of writing. They advocate teaching writing as a researchable subject of scholarly inquiry, an activity with its own content. Questioning the misconception that good writing is invariably the product of the "isolated, inspired writer" (561), the authors outline a set of classroom practices based on attainable goals, readings, and reflective assignments. It is, I believe, these attainable goals and assignments that make the authors' "Intro to Writing Studies" course one of the most compelling and applicable approaches to writing instruction published since composition's inception; however, these aims and assignments also make their curriculum highly vulnerable to critique.

In the end, the goal of Intro to Writing Studies is "to help students learn more about writing and become more successful writers in the university" (574). Yet, the authors readily admit that there is a fine line between this learning outcome and how those unfamiliar with the work of composition might interpret it. In other words, Intro to Writing Studies does not aim to teach students to be better writers in general, nor does it, as the authors write, "purport to do all that is necessary to prepare students to write in college" (559). Instead, it "promises to help students understand some activities related to written scholarly inquiry" (559) by introducing first-year writers to the research community of composition itself. There is much to admire about Downs's and Wardle's approach. From advocating a course of study that requires the guidance and direction of composition specialists specifically, to demystifying many of the myths that perpetuate complaints about composition today, Intro to Writing Studies does, indeed, offer a curriculum that aims to complicate persistent and tenacious assumptions about writing and students. Furthermore, that the authors have successfully parlayed the findings of "Teaching about Writing, Righting Misconceptions" into their successful 2011 textbook, *Writing about Writing*, is not only a testament to the accessibility and relevance of their findings, but also to the possibility that higher education is increasingly receptive to more progressive approaches to writing instruction.

However, despite the strengths of the Downs and Wardle approach, the success of the curriculum depends on the teaching of Intro to Writing Studies by specialists, a criticism the author's anticipate but, in my opinion, do not persuasively refute. They note:

> While faculty in other disciplines are expected to teach the content and methods of the fields even in the most introductory courses, many (if not most) FYC classes throughout the country allow students to write on any range of topics, topics which often fall outside the writing teachers' specialization. Writing teachers and students alike are better served by focusing specifically on topics teachers know. To argue otherwise accepts and perpetuates the myth that content is separable from writing—that an FYC instructor *need not be* expert in the subject matter of a paper in order to evaluate the quality of writing in that paper, or need not be a subject expert on writing in order to teach writing. Such claims accept the premise that writing instruction can be limited to fluent English syntax, grammar, and mechanics. (577)

Although I do not dispute the logic of this argument, it is difficult to imagine a time when specialists of composition studies alone will carry out the teaching of writing at most writing programs. After all, most graduate students teaching composition as part of pursuing an advanced degree in English studies (or a related discipline) are not credentialed or recognized as possessing "expertise" until they have completed their degree requirements. More often than not, writing programs find themselves in the difficult position of needing to prepare instructors unfamiliar with the nomenclature and conventions of composition studies to teach first-year writing. What is needed is a model of composition that makes the critical move proposed by Russell, Downs, and Wardle—shifting the focus of instructor preparation and the content of composition to learning to write *about* writing—but that does so from a perspective that offers a broader, more interdisciplinary framework that prepares students and instructors simultaneously to interrogate the idea of literacy altogether.

THE COMPULSORY COURSE IN FIRST-YEAR LITERACY STUDIES: LESSONS, OUTCOMES, AND QUESTIONS

In this section, I propose a series of lessons and learning outcomes that may be used to inform a course I call First-Year Literacy Studies (FYLS). To a great extent, what I assert here is indebted to concepts and questions raised by Russell ("Activity Theory") as well as Downs's and Wardle's Intro to Writing Studies curriculum. In a similar fashion, I am proposing that composition courses teach students to write about literacy rather than focus primarily on teaching them to become more literate in what Russell calls "universal educated discourse." However, unlike my predecessors, what I emphasize here is a model of composition that aspires to provide students *and* instructors with an orientation and language to participate in ongoing debates about the relevance of composition. While many view instructors' frustration with teaching composition and students' reluctance to take the course as an impediment to teacher preparation and student development, the truth is that anxieties and complaints about composition's effectiveness and purpose represent valid positions in an ongoing scholarly conversation. Further, as I show throughout *The Lure of Literacy*, what draws participants into the Great Debate over composition is not necessarily the design or aims of the composition course itself. Implicit and unacknowledged attitudes about and expectations related to literacy are the engine of the Great Debate over composition; these attitudes and expectations also function as the motivating force behind students and teachers' complaints about the course.

One way out of the ongoing debate over composition's purpose and effectiveness—or whether or not to make the course compulsory—is to include students and instructors in the debate itself. By reconceptualizing the debate over composition as a sort of laboratory in which teachers and students can work together to identify and test their own definitions of literacy against composition's staunchest critics, we create opportunities for providing students and teachers alike with a more sophisticated understanding of literacy and its complex role in the development of the very course they are required to teach or take. However, doing so without a conceptual framework indebted to literacy studies would only perpetuate the debate as it has persisted for over a century, and with the same results. In his fine study, *From Form to Meaning*, which deals with, among many things, the abolition of composition at the University of Wisconsin, David Fleming writes: "We are thus faced with the curious situation of the most widely required and taught undergraduate course in U.S. higher education backed by a professional community that no longer fully endorses it" (11). I believe this is the case because literacy remains something that—in composition studies specifically—we engage with anecdotally. Either because we believe that literacy is "well-traveled ground" in composition studies or because the task of understanding its relative pressures on composition pedagogy seems too great, we seem reluctant to insist that instructors employ more complex attitudes and characterizations of literacy in the composition classroom. Thus, what follows are lessons from the history of literacy and related learning outcomes intended to inform the development of a First-Year Literacy Studies Program (FYLS) that takes as its thematic commitment literacy studies and the ways complaints about the effectiveness and relevance of compulsory composition intersect with it. Lessons proposed in the following section come primarily from "Literacy, Myths, and Legacies: Lessons from the History of Literacy" in Harvey J. Graff's *The Labyrinths of Literacy*. These lessons are intended for FYLS students. Each lesson is accompanied by a related outcome, an objective informed by those that define the Ohio State University's Graduate Interdisciplinary Specialization in Literacy Studies.[2] Taken together, these lessons and outcomes are meant to function as a starting point for developing more precise learning objectives that deal explicitly with literacy for both students and instructors. Although I would like to propose that what follows is appropriate for every university writing program, I realize that institutional politics sometimes overlap with entrenched attitudes about literacy in ways that make educational reform difficult, especially reform toward the ends I describe in this book: using compulsory composition to interrogate the import, relevance, and nature of literacy. Therefore, each lesson and objective I propose is situated in a brief discussion, a context meant to raise the kinds of questions to be discussed in pedagogy forums and working groups, local initiatives that will, undoubtedly, make FYLS a more likely possibility.

Student Lesson I: Literacy is historical, and history teaches us there are many paths to literacy.

Among the most important lessons to be gleaned from contemporary participants in the Great Debate is that their frustrations, anxieties, and recommendations are not novel or new. However, just as critiques of composition are "historically founded and grounded" (Graff, *The Labyrinths of Literacy* 323), so too are the attitudes about literacy that motivate them. Stanley Fish's "What Should Colleges Teach?" is a revealing example of this lesson, and there are, as I and others have demonstrated, many other critiques of composition that have their roots in history. But there is much more to be learned from composition's critics than merely teaching those invested in composition that history is important or that it repeats itself. After all, as Graff states, "repetition is least among the costs of failing to learn from history; if only we might repeat the course!" (323). Graff's point about "repeating the course" has significant implications for understanding literacy and its role in the teaching of composition. It raises revealing questions about the reasons behind composition's lack of continuity in teaching practices and thematic commitments, and it encourages us to examine composition's course of inquiry for causes of disruption, distraction, or worse, willful ignorance.

Literacy crises place high on the list of the most disruptive forces in the development of a continuity of teaching practices in composition. Many scholars in composition have remarked on the ways that literacy crises have led to the development of compulsory composition.[3] Certainly, students and instructors would do well to recognize that formal composition instruction is, in many ways, a direct consequence of various literacy crises. However, there is something about the more general sense of crisis and urgency that seems to subsume discussions of literacy and composition with which students and teachers should be acquainted. Alice Brower's insistence that composition's aim is "to transform the chaos of today into a livable world tomorrow" is a fine example of this vague anxiety, as is Manchester's appropriation of religious rhetoric to describe the "demon of illiteracy" in his composition textbook. In both instances, understandings of composition's purpose are couched in an ambiguous sense of urgency meant to convey the relevance of literacy. And in both cases, as I demonstrated, this sense of crisis has paradoxical consequences: to narrow the vision of what is possible in the composition classroom, and more importantly, to reduce the various paths to literacy for students.

Teaching composition students this lesson begins with conveying to their instructors the importance of historical and comparative perspectives when examining literacy. I do not believe it is enough to teach students that when it comes to understanding literacy's past and present, "history repeats itself," or that the history of literacy is marked by confusion about the nature of literacy, or that what is remarkable about literacy's past is how much of it stays the same, especially with respect to continuities of crisis. These lessons are critical to the success of FYLS programs, but we must take the next step and teach literacy studies instructors that the "heightened sensitivity" (Graff, *The Labyrinths of Literacy* 321) associated with literacy crises must be situated historically and understood in specific contexts. As Shirley Brice Heath's *Ways With Words*, Deborah Brandt's *Literacy in American Lives*, and John Duffy's *Writing From These Roots* demonstrate, investigating literacy practices and events in specific contexts pays dividends on many levels, especially when it comes to understanding how literacy functions as both a foundation for schooling and democracy but is also a source of great inequity and anxiety. Key to understanding this point is recognizing that the heightened sensitivity that accompanies literacy crises serves to exacerbate and perpetuate inequity by narrowing our understanding of the many paths that people take to literacy. Exploring literacy in specific contexts—in ways indebted to Brandt, Duffy, Heath—provides powerful and more complicated images of people's "multiple paths of learning literacy" (*The Labyrinths of Literacy*, 328). Such images are the cornerstone of FYLS curriculum and are a critical component of instructor training programs aimed toward the following learning objective.

Instructor Learning Objective I: Recognize literacy in specific historical, social, cultural, political, and economic contexts.

Student Lesson II: Literacy is not simple.

Like many composition instructors, I build my courses around collaborative activities that ask students to define literacy in their own words, to work in groups to come to a consensus about that definition, and then to report their findings to the class. Students tend to define literacy in two ways: 1. As a thing that involves the dual activities of reading and writing; and 2. As a measurement of competence or aptitude related to a particular field of knowledge (e.g., "computer literacy," "financial literacy," etc.). While student definitions of literacy rarely explicitly state that literacy is easy or simple, the idea is implied, especially in the ways that students come to a consensus about their definitions of literacy. One thing that I have learned from collaborative activities that build toward consensus is that the knowledge that is socially constructed from deliberation and discussion is often less pedagogically useful than what we find when we examine the implied values that make consensus possible in the first place. When it comes to collaboratively defining literacy, I have found that it is students' shared investment in the powers of literacy to invariably lead to cognitive enhancement, intellectual transformation, and social affluence that makes shared definitions of literacy possible. That is, students' collective understandings of literacy often grow out of their abiding belief in the literacy myth. Collaborative activities like the one I have described may have the unintended effect of reinforcing attitudes about literacy that make the literacy myth even more entrenched. Nevertheless, the push to simplify understandings and definitions of literacy—the drive to get people "on the same page"—when it comes to defining literacy represents a narrowing of the paths to the historically and theoretically complex underpinnings of literacy. One of the principal lessons to be drawn from examining literacy in "specific historical, social, cultural, political, and economic contexts" (LS@OSU) is that definitions of literacy must be qualified and tied to historical particulars.

Graff asserts that the idea of "subjects such as literacy, learning, schooling, and education [as] simple, unproblematic notions is a further historical myth. Experience, historical and more recent, to the contrary jointly underscores their *fundamental complexity*—practically and theoretically" (324). As with the previous FYLS lesson ("Literacy is historical"), teaching students that literacy is fundamentally complex begins with teaching their instructors that the process of defining literacy is as much an opportunity for understanding the fundamental nature of literacy as it is a chance to talk about the limits of literacy—maybe even what literacy is not. Doing so depends heavily on instructors embracing the following objective.

Instructor Learning Objective II: Recognize that literacy cannot be reduced to one definition, nor to one effect on people or societies.

Student Lesson III: Literacy is not neutral or invariably good.

In the *Labyrinths of Literacy*, Graff writes: "To the contrary, *no mode* or *means of learning is neutral.* Not only does all 'knowledge,' however elementary, incorporate the assumptions and expectations, the biases of emphases of its production, association, prior use, maintenance, and preservation. So too do the so-called tools or skills" (326). Graff's statement challenges the commonsensical view of many composition students and instructors who assume that the stakes of the composition course are rooted in the innate goodness or neutrality of literacy. Further, Graff's remarks on the "tools or skills" of literacy also have broader implications for how we talk about literacy, which is a critical aspect of developing pedagogy aimed toward this student lesson and the related instructor objective.

Understanding that literacy is not neutral or invariably good does not mean providing evidence to the contrary (e.g., that literacy is "bad"). It also does not involve, as some might argue, asking students to re-imagine literacy altogether or to completely abandon personal understandings of literacy. In fact, an important part of learning that literacy is not neutral or invariably good involves drawing out and making more visible the language students use to define literacy and focusing on the tendency to oversimplify conceptions of it. An important part of investigating this impulse involves demonstrating that characterizations of literacy as neutral are often rooted in figurative expressions of literacy, specifically "skills-based" views of literacy.

In *Literacy: An Ecological Approach*, David Barton explains that this view of literacy presumes that it may be "broken down into a set of skills and subskills" (12). The essence of this view depends on the assumption that these subskills are sequentially ordered, and that to possess one skill means that previous skills (pre-reading or pre-writing) have been mastered. As a result, literacy is sometimes understood as a symptom of the various stages of this process, or as Barton puts it, "a psychological variable which can be measured and assessed" (12). As perhaps the most pervasive and influential view of literacy on reading programs and higher education, the skills-based perspective merits close attention by composition students because it demonstrates best how easy it is to forget that the way we talk about literacy affects how we view illiteracy. Barton reminds us that skills-based views of literacy are based on metaphors, and that they are no less figurative than characterizations of literacy based on metaphors of disease (12). Similar to disease metaphors, characterizing literacy from the skills-based perspective situates it as a psychological symptom, one that carries with it the expectation of therapy, counseling, or prescribed treatments as a remedy for the condition of illiteracy.

If this is the case, then major consequences follow for preparing instructors to teach students that the metaphors we use to discuss literacy determine the pedagogical approaches we develop, as well as the models of thinking we presume students possess. But asking instructors to investigate with their students the figurative underpinnings of attitudes about literacy is not enough. Instructors of FYLS must understand that the implications of how we talk about literacy reach to other contexts. Just as problematic as disease and skills-based metaphors in understandings of literacy are other uses, abuses, and contradictions that stem from presuming that literacy is neutral or invariably related to the good. On this point, Graff notes: "Structures of authority are erected on these bases and lines as certain forms of literacy and language abilities support social differentiation, social stigmatization, reinforcement of inequality—and school failure among the young, and not so young" (Graff, *The Labyrinths of Literacy* 327). Graff suggests that such failures are linked to "literate biases" (327), or characterizations, definitions, and attitudes about literacy that often bring about "contradictions in literacy's and education's history" (326).

As I have shown throughout *The Lure of Literacy*, the history of the debate over composition's relevance and effectiveness teaches us that attempts to reform composition—even with the best intentions—sometimes have the contradictory effect of reinforcing attitudes about literacy that make stigmatization of students and inequality more likely. Such failures are directly linked with the way we talk about and understand literacy. What is needed are more useful, relevant, and specific understandings of literacy, characterizations of learning that grow not from "legacies of received wisdom" (326), but from investigations of literacy in specific social practices and contexts. With these aims in mind, I propose that instructors of FYLS are best prepared to help students reformulate understandings of literacy, when they themselves embrace the following objective.

Instructor Learning Objective III: Investigate the uses, abuses, complexity, and contradictions of literacy as a social practice.

Student Lesson IV: The consequences of literacy are curious.

A key pedagogical strategy for encouraging students to become more curious about rhetoric involves teaching students about its ancient and historical underpinnings. Pedagogical approaches emphasizing historical receptions of rhetoric are effective because they provide students with a more complex frame of reference for the term than popular conceptions. Students learn that rhetoric has multiple definitions, uses, and theoretical suppositions—that it is constituted by many devices, but more importantly, that it has developed a tradition over time, and that this tradition is comprised of both discontinuities and continuities. This context frequently leads students to be genuinely curious about rhetoric's past. It is a lesson we teach them so that they might appropriate rhetorical precepts from the rhetorical tradition and employ relevant aspects of rhetoric in their everyday lives.

One aim of a course in FYLS is to promote a similar sense of curiousness about literacy. Although students frequently come to writing courses mystified by academic discourse, uncertain about grammatical practices, and often possessing pejorative and superficial understandings of rhetoric, literacy is something that many students talk about with great confidence. And while they might struggle with the task of articulating definitions of literacy, their attitudes about it are often unwavering, especially when it comes to discussing the consequences that come from possessing it. To put it bluntly, for many students, literacy is merely synonymous with power and status. From this perspective, literacy raises the literate and the written to the status of the dominant, more intellectual—and even more human—partner in what Ruth Finnegan and others have called the "Great Divide" (Graff, *The Labyrinths of Literacy* 327). As such, literacy does not merit further curiosity or warrant ongoing investigation or examination. After all, if literacy elevates a person to the dominant position in a host of dichotomies—light/dark, civilization/barbarity, developed/primitive, formally schooled/natural, written/spoken, literate/oral (327)—then what is there to be curious about? Sometimes finding a way of not ending up on the "wrong" side of an ethnocentric, arrogant, and imperialistic interpretation of the world outweighs intellectual curiosity.

Unfortunately, many composition students are well aware of what it means to be the dominated partner in such dichotomies because of their experiences with strong theories of literacy in compulsory schooling more generally. As I discussed in chapter 1, Mike Rose's "Narrowing the Mind and Page: Remedial Writers and Cognitive Reductionism" discusses problems that arise from grand dichotomies and "great divide" characterizations of literacy, attitudes that are linked to strong theories of literacy. Generalizations based on strong theories of literacy lead to conceptions of students that we see throughout the history of the great debate (especially in Lounsbury, Campbell, Manchester, and Lange). Composition students are seen as lacking the ability to think analytically or abstractly about the world, or in Rose's words, they are "thought to bear cognitive resemblance to (ethnocentric notions of) primitive tribesmen in remote third-world cultures" (346). And while the development and growth of modern composition studies in the last 40 years has done much to complicate and change such views of students and basic writers, essays like Stanley Fish's "What Should Colleges Teach?" suggest there is still much work to be done. This work, I believe, can and should be carried out by instructors *and* students in FYLS courses, but the success of this work depends on our willingness to be intellectually curious about literacy in composition and to resist the tendency to only think of literacy in terms of the ostensible consequences that come from possessing it.

Voices and participants in the Great Debate over composition provide many opportunities for students to see and—because students are often the targets of these diatribes—*experience* strong theories of literacy in action. However, the purpose of explicating these texts for literate biases, strong theories of literacy, great divide conceptions, and myths is not to deny the profound influence or value of literacy to students. On the contrary, literacy is profoundly complex and important, so critical that the task of composition courses should be to encourage, complicate, and cultivate students' curiosity about literacy *and* literacy studies. More importantly, FYLS courses should teach students to engage in inquiry that questions the extent to which reductive and commonsensical theories of literacy can accurately evaluate and describe the consequences of being literate.

Doing so, of course, means first asking instructors to revisit their own experiences as student writers, and to interpret those experiences through the lenses of the New Literacy Studies. One potentially useful platform for doing this work is the Digital Archive of Literacy Narratives (DALN). A web-based, publicly available archive of personal literacy narratives in a variety of formats (text, video, audio), the DALN functions as a historical record of the literacy practices and values of contributors, as those practices and values change. The DALN "invites people of all ages, races, communities, backgrounds, and interests to contribute stories about how—and in what circumstances—they read, write, and compose meaning, and how they learned to do so (or helped others learn)." What is so pedagogically valuable about the DALN in particular is that it provides the opportunity not only to explore literacy in specific contexts—a chief aim and defining characteristic of the New Literacy Studies—and it also allows users to see how attitudes, definitions, and expectations of literacy are shaped by gender, ethnicity, class, race, and geography. Further, because the site is comprised of narratives in a variety of forms (alphabetic, audio, and video), it also provides opportunities for students to see how various composing mediums constrain and expand the process of characterizing the centrality of literacy in people's lives.

But there are other points to be noted about the pedagogical value of the DALN. Indeed, the DALN provides a valuable historical record of people's experiences with literacy. However, I believe the archive is perhaps most useful for persuading students that literacy deserves greater critical attention—that they should be more curious about its consequences. There may be no better way to persuade students of this fact than by asking instructors to work alongside students to contribute to the DALN. Developing assignments along these lines, in which students learn from their instructors' contributions to the archive, will create pedagogical environments in which students will be more likely to do the difficult work of expanding *and* critiquing the centrality of literacy in our current cultural moment.

Instructor Learning Objective IV: Study the acquisition, uses, practices, and consequences of literacy and literacies across age, gender, race, class, ethnicity, geography, and media.

Student Lesson V: The literacy myth does not express a falsehood.

Harvey J. Graff and John Duffy define the literacy myth as "the belief, articulated in educational, civic, religious, and other settings, contemporary and historical, that the acquisition of literacy is a necessary precursor to and invariably results in economic development, democratic practice, cognitive enhancement, and upward social mobility" (35). The authors note that despite attempts to measure the consequence of possessing literacy, the term carries with it "immeasurable and indeed almost ineffable qualities," providing literate people and societies a "predilection toward social order, an elevated moral sense, and a metaphorical 'state of grace'" (35). Also related to the purported powers of literacy is the idea that the "benefits ascribed to literacy cannot be attained in other ways, nor can they be attributed to other factors, whether economic, political, cultural, or individual." In sum, "literacy stands alone as the independent and critical variable" (35).

There are many pedagogical challenges involved with teaching students about the literacy myth. Merely raising the possibility of the existence of the literacy myth sometimes invites calls for "proof," evidence that disproves perceived correlations among literacy and economic prosperity, psychological enhancement, intellectual aptitude, and a host of other consequences. However, it is important that students and instructors alike remember that "Like all myths," as Graff writes in "The Literacy Myth at Thirty," the "literacy myth is not so much a falsehood but an expression of the ideology of those who sanction it and are invested in its outcomes" (638). Certainly, as I have shown throughout *The Lure of Literacy*, examining proposals to abolish and reform composition provides opportunities for exploring the relationship between the literacy myth and the criticisms that are lobbed at the course. Moreover, because literacy myths depend heavily on vague definitions and characterizations of literacy, writing assignments that make use of the Great Debate hold the potential to teach students important lessons about how definitions of literacy sustain and perpetuate the myth. After all, it is only by grounding "definitions of literacy in specific, qualified, and historical particulars" that we "avoid conferring upon it the status of myth" (*The Literacy Myth at Thirty*, 639). Nevertheless, teaching students perhaps the most important lesson to be learned about the literacy myth—that it is not so much an expression of falsehood as a representation of the ideology of people who gain from others investing in it—requires, I believe, more timely and local contexts. Students must understand that literacy myths are at play in their everyday lives and that myths thrive, in many cases, in unexpected places.

For instance, in August of 2008, the Columbus Blue Jackets, a professional hockey team based in Columbus, Ohio, announced that Time Warner Cable had named their team captain, Rick Nash, to be the spokesman for Time Warner's annual month-long adult literacy campaign. Previous spokespersons for the campaign include former NFL football star and Heisman Trophy winner Eddie George; Indianapolis 500 champion Bobby Rahal; and former heavyweight champion boxer George Foreman. During the campaign, Time Warner Cable donates a portion of cable installation fees to adult literacy programs in the Mid-Ohio region (Columbus Blue Jackets). According to Rhonda Fraas, Time Warner Cable's Mid-Ohio Division president, "More than 500,000 adults in Central Ohio don't have the necessary skills to read, write or function effectively in society." Commenting on the impact of donations to the program, Fraus notes, "Every penny donated to help someone learn to read is money well invested. Our Adult Literacy Campaign has been successful in raising critical funds with the help of prominent spokespersons like Rick Nash. We appreciate their support."

Promotional materials for the campaign include press releases that report, among other items, funds raised since the inception of the campaign in 1990 (over $500,000), as well as print collateral with pictures of spokespersons. For the 2008 campaign, Rick Nash's picture is prominently displayed on a promotional item meant to look like a book cover. He is dressed in a Columbus Blue Jacket uniform, holding a hockey stick and leaning against a goal. Above his head is a caption that reads, "Knowing How To Read Can Take You Anywhere." The back of the cover, meant to appear as a title of a book, states: "How To Score A Goal For Adult Literacy by: Rick Nash and you." In addition, the "book" appears to have been through many editions, as there is a medallion on the cover positioned next to a skating Rick Nash that reads, "19th edition—Countless Success Stories!"

When readers open the book cover, they find three panels. On the left side is a short paragraph by Time Warner. In addition to reporting that they have donated $558,000 to Ohio literacy providers since 1990, they also articulate the stakes of their campaign. They write: "But there is still more work to be done. Right now, there are people in your own community who struggle to read a magazine. They can't fill out a job application, understand the instructions on a prescription label, or read to their children. In fact, there are more than 500,000 adults in Mid-Ohio who don't have the necessary skills to read, write, or function effectively in society. Please join us in the 'Score a Goal' campaign to fight adult illiteracy. Because word by word, we're changing lives" (Read). The panel on the right includes another image of Rick Nash, again in his hockey uniform, holding an open book with a short quote that is superimposed over a diluted logo of Time Warner Cable. The quote states: "It's Never Too Late to Learn to Read!" This image, and others like it, is particularly revealing and instructive when it comes to teaching students about the literacy myth because, again, the pedagogical aim of providing students more critical frameworks for talking about literacy is not to teach them that literacy is unimportant. Instead, the goal is to teach them that the literacy myth elides latent ideologies that depend on vague and commonsensical attitudes about literacy to circulate. In sum, there is something behind our collective investment in the literacy myth.

In the case of the Time Warner literacy campaign this fact is best demonstrated when readers peruse the middle panel of the promotional item. Here, readers find the true intent behind the "Score a Goal" initiative: to gain subscribers for Timer Warner Cable's digital phone service. It states: "Help someone learn to read with this great offer! Get 2 months FREE Digital Phone Service. $5 of your installation fee will be donated to local literacy providers." Particularly noteworthy is the fine print which states that this is a "limited time offer," that the installation fee is $9.95, and for what it is worth, the free service only applies to the 6th and 12th months; thus, subscribers should be prepared to wait "45 days to receive 6th and 12th month rebate coupons by mail" (Read). However, even more significant is the fact that in 2008 the "Score a Goal" campaign was recognized by the Cable & Telecommunications Association with a Mark Award, an honor that recognizes outstanding achievement and excellence in marketing. In a "Marketing Summary" made available by the Mark Awards committee, Time Warner candidly states the intent behind the campaign: "Our goal was to use a variety of media to persuade our audience to purchase a Triple Play bundled package, including Digital Cable, Road Runner High-Speed Online and Digital Phone Service, with our commitment to donate a portion of the install fee to local literacy providers" (Mark Awards). According to the summary, Time Warner's literacy campaign, which relied on a "heavy media schedule and attractive creative" and required a total marketing budget of $82,000, enabled the company to gain 10,855 new customers.

What is so valuable about the "Score a Goal" campaign is that it demonstrates the multifaceted nature of the literacy myth and the ways in which characterizations of literacy depend heavily on the perceived consequences of possessing it. At bottom, the implied image of the nonliterate person in this campaign is someone who is unable to be entertained because s/he cannot read a magazine; who is unemployable because s/he cannot fill out a job application; who is a bad parent because s/he cannot read to their children; who is unhealthy because s/he cannot read a prescription. Of course, what we know about literate adults is that entertainment can be hard to come by and that the ability to read and write does not necessarily translate into gainful employment or good parenting. Simply put, literacy myths (and strong theories of literacy more generally) do not accurately describe or account for the effects of possessing literacy, nor does Rick Nash, Time Warner Cable, or Stanley Fish for that matter. In appealing to the general public's collective and abiding belief in the myth, Time Warner perpetuates conceptions of literacy that erect erroneous divides between the literate and nonliterate. Such dichotomies have little to do with providing wider access to literacy instruction or its ostensible benefits, but function instead to artificially elevate the literate over the nonliterate in ethnocentric and condescending ways. The implicit message here is that nonliterate adults cannot "Score a Goal" in life; only the literate get this chance, only they can be effective in society.

At base, the task of instructors in FYLS programs is to identify other contemporary examples that draw on literacy myths and great divide conceptions of learning and to situate these primary sources historically and comparatively. Though I concede that there are other undergraduate curriculums that ask students to make similar moves, I still insist that the pedagogical value of such courses would be enhanced if they were sanctioned by FYLS programs that take as their focus both the complaints and criticisms of composition that sustain the Great Debate and contemporary examples of the literacy myth in action. Ultimately, what is at stake is teaching students that contemporary examples of the literacy myth share profound similarities with the criticisms, concerns, and anxieties that students and instructors possess about compulsory composition. Teaching students these valuable lessons means first encouraging instructors to develop lesson plans and learning outcomes aimed toward the final FYLS Instructor Objective.

Instructor Learning Objective V: Develop critical approaches to common assumptions about the importance, power, and centrality of literacy.

Taken together these lessons and objectives are intended to realize a more general goal of the FYLS curriculum: Encouraging students and instructors to reflect on why we, as a society, ask so much of literacy. In *National Literacy Campaigns in Historical and Comparative Perspective*, Arnove and Graff write: "To ask of literacy that it overcome gender discrimination, integrate a society, eliminate inequalities, and contribute to political and social stability is certainly too much" (27). *The Lure of Literacy*, then, is meant to promote the development of writing programs that recognize that coming to terms with the literacy myth might mean placing a greater emphasis on *how* we work together both intentionally and unintentionally to position literacy as an independent variable in culture. Furthermore, this book contends that it is by working alongside our students to investigate, explore—and, yes, rhetorically analyze—the images, tropes, figures, and institutions that give voice to the literacy myth that we come to understand how our latent and collective desires inform our susceptibility to the rhetoric and lure of literacy. Thirty years after the publication of Harvey Graff's *The Literacy Myth* we know now that literacy myths are particularly resilient (certainly as resilient as the ideologies that make them possible). As such, it is safe to claim that the literacy myth is here to stay, and it is quite possible that we need it—or at least the field of Composition and Rhetoric must act as if it does. But there are good reasons for this, as Harvey Graff notes in "The Literacy Myth at Thirty": "Perhaps the Literacy Myth expresses a hope that literacy alone is enough to end poverty, elevate human dignity, and ensure a just and democratic world. A less benign reading is that the Literacy Myth is a means through which to obscure the causes of social and economic inequities in Western society at least by attributing them to the literacy or illiteracy of different peoples" (645). As such, it may be impossible for our field to lose, transcend, or explode the literacy myth and retain our position in higher education. As I and others have asserted, the myth plays a substantial role in how we articulate our relevance to those who have a stake in compulsory composition, even those scholars who have made careers out of criticizing it. Our only choice, it seems, is to embrace the literacy myth and redirect it as a site of inquiry and hope that by doing so we might complicate and clarify our own and students' understandings of it (652). Indeed, coming to terms with the literacy myth for composition means recognizing that it is ever-present in the everyday work of our profession, and that we are no longer in a position to turn a blind eye to it. Doing so, in the form of compulsory FYLS programs, will remake the field of composition along more progressive and equitable lines and demonstrate once and for all, especially to our critics, that we are, in fact, literate ourselves.

NOTES

INTRODUCTION

1. Warner G. Rice touches on each of these complaints in his article, "A Proposal for the Abolition of Freshman English, As It Is Now Commonly Taught, from the College Curriculum. See pages 361–362 for his explications.

2. It is important to note that Connors never had the opportunity to expand his study into a prolonged investigation of the topic. "The New Abolitionism: Toward a Historical Background" began as a conference paper and was presented at the 1993 conference on "Composition in the Twenty-first Century: Crisis and Change." A condensed version of the presentation appeared in the volume of papers for that conference. Then, a slightly longer version appeared in Petraglia's *Reconceiving Writing, Rethinking Writing Instruction*. Following Connors's tragic death in June of 2000, his study was revised and anthologized in the *Selected Essays of Robert J. Connors* and renamed, "The Abolition Debate in Composition: A Short History."

3. Maureen Daly Goggin and Susan Kay Miller chracterize the controversy over compulsory composition as the "Great Debate." See "What is *New* About the 'New Abolitionists': Continuities and Discontinuities in the Great Debate" for a more complete discussion of this expression. In my study, the "Tradition of Complaint," the "Great Debate," and the "debate over compulsory composition" are used interchangeably. However, in my fourth chapter, I draw a distinction between general complaints about the aims and effectiveness of composition and specific polemics (like Sharon Crowley's) that call for the abolition of the *universal requirement* of composition. Along similar lines, "Freshman English," "freshman composition," "composition," and "first-year writing" are also used interchangeably, not because I am ignoring the well-established fact that composition courses vary considerably across time, regions, and historical contexts, but because I aim to create continuity between how I and subjects of my analysis refer to the course.

4. My use of the expression, "legacies of literacy" is indebted to Harvey J. Graff's *The Labyrinths of Literacy: Reflections on Literacy Past and Present*. In "Literacy, Myths, and Legacies: Lessons from the History of Literacy" (pp. 318–349) he writes: "The 'strong theory' of literacy—despite its hold on popular and policy opinions—turns out to be much weaker, with literacy's impacts seldom so direct, unmediated, abstract, or universal. Constituting much of what I call literacy's central contradictions, these legacies taken together constitute 'the literacy myth,' a powerful force despite its massive criticism and rejection in some circles" (324).

CHAPTER ONE

1. Studies in composition dealing with the topic of critical literacy and pedagogy are too numerous to account for in this book. However, some of the most important include: James Berlin's "Freirean Pedagogy in the U.S.: A Response"; Wendy Bishop's "Because Teaching Composition Is (Still) Mostly about Teaching Composition"; Patricia Bizzell's *Academic Discourse and Critical Consciousness*; Lil Brannon's and C. H. Knoblauch's *Critical Teaching and the Idea of Literacy*; Marilyn Cooper's "We Don't Belong Here, Do We? A Response to Lives on the Boundary and The Violence of Literacy"; Ellen Cushman's "The Public Intellectual, Service Learning, and Activist Research" and "The Rhetorician as an Agent of Social Change"; Sidney Dobrin's "Paralogic Hermeneutic Theories, Power, and the Possibility of for Liberating Pedagogies"; Elizabeth Ellsworth's *Teaching Positions: Difference, Pedagogy, and the Power of Address*; Stephen Fishman's and Lucille Parkinson McCarthy's "*John Dewey and the Challenge of Classroom Practice*; Chris Gallagher's *Radical Departures: Composition and Progressive Pedagogy*; James Paul Gee's "Progressivism, Critique, and Socially Situated Minds"; Keith Gilyard's "Composition and the Critical Moment"; Henry A. Giroux's "Authority, Intellectuals, and the Politics of Practical Learning" and *Ideology, Culture, and the Process of Schooling*; Jeff Grabill's *Community Literacy Programs and the Politics of Change*; Joe Marshill Hardin's *Opening Spaces: Critical Pedagogy and Resistance Theory in Composition*; bell hooks's *Teaching to Transgress: Education as the Practice of Freedom*; Susan Kates's *Activist Rhetorics and American Higher Education: 1885–1937*; Min-Zhan Lu's and Bruce Horner's "The Problematic of Experience: Redefining Critical Work in Ethnography and Pedagogy;" Donald Murray's "Finding Your Own Voice: Teaching Composition in the Age of Dissent;" Gary A. Olson's "History, Praxis, and Change: Paulo Freire and the Politics of Literacy;" Mike Rose's *An Open Language: Selected Writing on Literacy, Learning, and Opportunity*; David Seitz's "Hard Lessons Learned Since the First Generation of Critical Pedagogy;" Ira Shor's *Critical Teaching and Everyday Life*; Geoffrey Sirc's *English Composition as a Happening*; and Victor Villanueva's *Bootstraps: From an American Academic of Color*.

2. See Nan Johnson's *Nineteenth-Century Rhetoric in North America*; James L. Golden's and Edward P. J. Corbett's *The Rhetoric of Blair, Campbell, and Whately*; and H. Lewis Ulman's *Things, Thoughts, Words, and Actions: The Problem of Language in Late Eighteenth-Century British Rhetorical Theory*. See also Lynée Lewis Gaillet's and Thomas P. Miller's study, "Making Use of the Nineteenth Century: The Writings of Robert Connors and Recent Histories of Rhetoric and Composition."

3. See John C. Brereton's *The Origins of Composition Studies in the American College, 1875–1925* (pp. 31–33) for a fine history on the origins of theme writing in college composition.

4. In *The Origins of Composition Studies in the American College, 1875–1925*, Brereton writes: "Of all the complex factors that influenced the university's formation, four stand out: the influence of the German university model, the changing nature of knowledge, the dramatic expansion of higher education, and the efforts of a few visionaries to update the university's purview. All of these factors were to shatter traditional rhetoric and to aid in the emergence of modern composition" (5).

5. It is important to note that Veysey's interpretation of "the rise" of the university has been criticized. There is now a more nuanced understanding that draws less on notions of "revolutions/revolutionary change." Class, gender, and culture, as well as ethnicity and race, all in relationships to education and social change, are among the historical dynamics shaping the changes and efforts to respond to them driving this history of higher education. However, Veysey's discussion of academic specialization specifically is the most pertinent aspect of his work for this study.

6. See James A. Berlin's *Rhetoric and Reality: Writing Instruction in American Colleges, 1900–1985*; Maurice R. Berube's *American School Reform: Progressive, Equity, and Excellence Movements, 1883–1993*; John C. Brereton's *The Origins of Composition Studies in the American College, 1875–1925: A Documentary History*; Robert J. Connors's *Composition-Rhetoric: Backgrounds, Theory, and Pedagogy*; Frederick Rudolph's *The American College & University*; and Laurence R. Veysey's *The Emergence of the American University*.

7. See Robert J. Connors's "The New Abolitionism" for a discussion of these responses (pp. 8–9). See also F. A. Dudley's "The Success of Freshman English" and A. J. Green's "The Reform of Freshman English" for responses to Campbell's "The Failure of Freshman English."

8. In "Romantics on Writing" Russell contends that advocates of liberal culture "were elitist, suspicious of the democratic reforms sweeping the university, particularly rising enrollments and the specialized elective curriculum. They saw these as a threat to the standards of taste that liberal culture defended—often with terms borrowed from social darwinists" (133). Drawing from Veysey's *The Emergence of the American University*, Russell understands liberal culture to have been highly invested in the "Arnoldian ideal of the 'well-rounded man,'" a person with "a wide vision of the best things which man has done or aspired after" (qtd. in Russell 133; Veysey 186).

9. It is important to note that Rose's "The Language of Exclusion: Writing Instruction at the University" does not deal with the abolition debate specifically. Rather, Rose's seminal study takes up (among other notable currents in higher education) the history of remediation. See pages 598–603 for Rose's complete discussion of the myth of transience. See also David Fleming's *From Form to Meaning: Freshman Composition and the Long Sixties, 1957–1974* for a fine discussion of Rose's essay (pp. 8–10).

10. Perhaps his snarkiest remark appears on p. 179 when he writes: "Never mind, we answer, say your nothing anyway, and mind that you say it in perfectly punctuated sentences, phrases, clauses, and paragraphs. If you continue thus to express your vacancy, by the end of the year you will know how to write anything and everything."

CHAPTER TWO

1. Unlike Barton's figure, Kenneth Levine's table in *The Social Context of Literacy* does not contain a row for "oppression." Barton's revision presumably refers to Paulo Freire's understanding of literacy articulated in *The Pedagogy of the Oppressed*.

2. For a discussion of classification discourse and the ways that the "modes of discourse" have influenced the history of writing instruction see Robert J. Connors's "The Rise and Fall of the Modes of Discourse."

3. The American Library Association Publishing Board's *A.L.A. Booklist: The Guide to the Best New Books* contains the following entry for this text (Thurber's essay contains no bibliographic information): "A classed list of books and periodical articles, covering the importance of good English to engineers, the teaching of English to engineering students, and the composition of engineering papers. Appended is a list of recommended engineering books. Includes no titles later than January, 1916. The compiler's *Handbook of English for engineers* (Scott, Foresman, 1913, 314p., $1.50 net, 13–1625) is one of the best of its type." The *Handbook of English for engineers* is cross-referenced as "Rhetoric—Bibliography" and "Engineering—Bibliography."

4. It is important to mention that David Fleming mentions Frederick A. Manchester in his book, *From Form to Meaning: Freshman Composition and the Long Sixties, 1957–1974*. Fleming links Manchester to a publication by the University of Wisconsin's Department of English titled, "Instructions to Students in Freshman English." A search of the WorldCat Identities Database (Beta version) and the Library of Congress Authority File (or the Online Computer Library Center) notes that Frederick A. Manchester, "formerly of the University of Wisconsin," and author of "Composition for College Students" was born Dec. 31 1882, and died in August of 1974. I emphasize Manchester's biographical information here because his discussion of the "demon of illiteracy" in his 1948 co-authored textbook is key to the assertions I make about the development of Manchester's attitudes about literacy over time.

5. Evidence that Manchester is responsible for this section may be found in the Preface to the fifth edition. It reads: "Mr. Thomas assumes primary responsibility for Chapters III, IV, VII, VIII, and IX; Mr. Manchester for Chapters I, V, and X: Mr. Manchester and Mr. Scott for Chapter II (the present revisions is the work of Mr. Scott); Mr. Scott for Chapter VI and the Handbook." The title page of the fifth edition (published in New York by The Macmillan Company) in 1948 lists Frederick A. Manchester "formerly of the University of Wisconsin" as one of the co-authors of the text.

6. Writing in the late 1960s, Manchester emphatically states his position on the importance of religion in education. In "Moral Education and History" (published July 1968 in *The Freeman*) he writes: "It leads to the conclusion that an imperative requirement of our time is an all-out drive toward intensifying the moralizing activities of the home, the church, and all other relevant social agencies, and the establishment, at all levels, of a definite plan of moral education, wherever it does not now exist, in our educational institutions. To ignore this requirement, in view of the world outlook of the moment, and especially of the consequent urgent demand for political and other leaders trained, not merely technically, but pre-eminently for wisdom and character, might seem to reasonably prudent minds to verge on madness."

CHAPTER THREE

1. On this matter Harvey J. Graff writes, "Even elementary literacy as learned and practiced is quite complex physiologically, neurologically, and cognitively. Its social and cultural dimensions add on numerous layers of complex meanings—among

them 'continuities and contradictions,' as I term them. How little we know about learning—and about teaching, too, especially respecting the level of literacy" (*The Labyrinths of Literacy*, 324).

2. Representatives from the following colleges participated on the committee: Adrian College, Albion College, Alma College, Aquinas College, Bay City Junior College, Central Michigan College of Education, Emmanuel Missionary College, Flint Junior College, Grand Rapids Junior College, Highland Park Junior College, Hillsdale College, Hope College, Jackson Junior College, Kalamazoo College, Marygrove College, Michigan College of Mining and Technology, Michigan State College of Agriculture and Applied Science, Michigan State Normal College, Muskegon Junior College, Nazareth College, Northern Michigan College of Education, Port Huron Junior College, Siena Heights College, Spring Arbor Seminary and Junior College, St. Mary's College, University of Detroit, University of Michigan, Wayne University, and Western Michigan College of Education.

CHAPTER FOUR

1. It is important to note that Connors names Crowley's 1991 study, "A Personal Essay on Freshman English" as the founding statement of new abolitionism. However, her essay was reprinted in *Composition in the University*.

CHAPTER FIVE

1. However, Fish does point out that "as a matter of law students have the right to any dialect they choose to deploy"—hardly surprising, as he is a law professor.

2. The Graduate Interdisciplinary Specialization (GIS) in Literacy Studies is an initiative of Literacy Studies@OSU (LS@OSU). Founded by Harvey J. Graff in 2004, LS@OSU's mission is "to foster a critical, cross-campus conversation and collaborative investigation into the nature of literacy, bringing together historical, contextual, comparative, and critical perspectives and modes of understanding, from the social and natural sciences to the arts and humanities, education, medicine, and law, stimulating new institutional and intellectual relationships between different disciplinary clusters and their constituents" (LS@OSU). While the FYLS curriculum lists five instructor objectives, the GIS in Literacy Studies includes nine goals. They are listed below as they appear on the LS@OSU website:

- Understanding literacy in its specific historical, social, cultural, political, and economic contexts
- Recognizing that the origins of literacy lie in language and the uses of language vary from context to context
- Exploring literacy's place in cognition and communication, and in relation to other modes of communicative competence
- Studying acquisition, uses, practices, and consequences of literacy and literacies across age, gender, race, class, ethnicity, geography, and media

- Evaluating, critiquing, and redeveloping communication and understanding across different literacies
- Investigating the uses, abuses, complexity, and contradictions of literacy as a social practice
- Developing critical approaches to common assumptions about the importance, power, and centrality of literacy
- Distinguishing and evaluating the literacies of academic disciplines for their commonalities and differences
- Critiquing and redeveloping communication and understanding across different literacies
- Recognizing that literacy cannot be reduced to one definition, nor to one effect on people or societies.

3. See especially Robert Connors's "The New Abolitionism" and David R. Russell's *Writing in the Academic Disciplines: A Curricular History*.

WORKS CITED

A.L.A. *Booklist: The Guide to the Best New Books*. Boston: American Library Association Publishing Board, 1916. Print.

Abbot, Andrew. *The Chaos of Disciplines*. Chicago: U of Chicago P, 2001. Print.

Alter, Stephen G. *William Dwight Whitney and the Science of Language*. Baltimore: Johns Hopkins UP, 2005. Print.

Applebee, Arthur N. *Tradition and Reform in the Teaching of English: A History*. Urbana, IL: NCTE, 1974. Print.

Arnove, Robert F., and Harvey Graff, eds. *National Literacy Campaigns in Historical and Comparative Perspective*. New York: Plenum, 1987. Print.

Austin, Allen. "The Abolition of Freshman Composition." *College English*. 22 (1961): 507. Print.

Bain, Alexander. *English Composition and Rhetoric: A Manual*. London: Longmans, 1866. Print.

Bartholomae, David. "Composition, 1900–2000." *PMLA*. 115.7 (2000): 1950–54. Print.

Barton, David. *Literacy: An Introduction to the Ecology of Written Language*. Malden, MA: Blackwell, 1994. Print.

Bazerman, Charles. "Response: Curricular Responsibilities and Professional Definition." Petraglia 249–59. Charles Bazerman, and David R. Russell, eds. *Landmark Essays on Writing Across the Curriculum*. Anaheim, CA: Hermagoras, 1994. Print.

Berlin, James A. *Rhetoric and Reality: Writing Instruction in American Colleges, 1900–1985*. Carbondale: Southern Illinois UP, 1987. Print.

———. "Freirean Pedagogy in the U.S.: A Response." *Journal of Advanced Composition* 12Q.2 (1992): 414–21. Print.

Berube, Maurice R. *American School Reform: Progressive, Equity, and Excellence Movements, 1883–1993*. Westport, CT: Praeger, 1994. Print.

Beyer, Thomas Percival. "Anent Compulsory Composition in Colleges." *Educational Review* 44 (1912): 77–86. Print.

Binkeley, Harold C. "If the Salt Have Lost Its Savor." *Journal of Higher Education* 11 (1940): 182–88. Print.

Bishop, Wendy. "Because Teaching Composition Is (Still) Mostly about Teaching Composition." *Composition Studies in the New Millennium: Rereading the Past, Rewriting the Future*. By Lynn Z. Bloom, Donald A. Daiker, and Edward M. White. Carbondale: Southern Illinois UP, 2003. 65–77. Print.

Bizzell, Patricia, and Bruce Herzberg, eds. *The Rhetorical Tradition: Readings from Classical Times to the Present*. New York: Bedford/St. Martin's, 2001. Print.

———. *Academic Discourse and Critical Consciousness*. Pittsburgh: University of Pittsburgh, 1992. Print.

Brandt, Deborah. *Literacy in American Lives*. New York: Cambridge UP, 2001. Print.

Brandt, Deborah, and Katie Clinton. "Limits of the Local: Expanding Perspectives on Literacy as a Social Practice." *The Norton Book of Composition Studies*. Ed. Susan Miller. New York: Norton, 2009. Print.

Brereton, John C., ed. *The Origins of Composition Studies in the American College, 1875–1925: A Documentary History*. Pittsburgh: U of Pittsburgh P, 1995. Print.

Brower, Alice V. "Problems of High-School English and College Freshman English." *College English* 3.8 (1942) 725–34. Print.

Burke, Kenneth. *Permanence and Change: An Anatomy of Purpose*. 3rd ed. Berkeley: U of California P, 1996. Print.

———. *A Rhetoric of Motives*. Berkeley: U of California P, 1969. Print.

Campbell, Oscar James. "The Failure of Freshman English." *English Journal* coll. ed. 28 (1939): 177–85. Print.

———. *The Teaching of College English*. New York: Appleton-Century, 1934. Print.

Carter, Chris. "Marketing Excellence in Higher Education." *Education as Civic Engagement: Toward a More Democratic Society*. Eds. Gary A. Olson and Lynn Worsham. New York: Palgrave Macmillan, 2012. Print.

Coffey, Daniel P. "A Discipline's Composition: A Citation Analysis of Composition Studies." *Journal of Academic Librarianship* 32.2 (Mar. 2006): 155–165. Digital.

Columbus Blue Jackets. "Blue Jackets Captain Rick Nash is New Time Warner Cable Literacy Spokesperson." Web. 10 Aug. 2011.

Conference on College Composition and Communication (CCCC). "Students' Right to Their Own Language." *College Composition and Communication* 25 (1974). Print.

Connors, Robert J. "The Abolition Debate in Composition: A Short History." Ede and Lunsford 279–94'

———. *Composition-Rhetoric: Backgrounds, Theory, and Pedagogy*. Pittsburgh: U of Pittsburgh P, 1997. Print.

———. "The New Abolitionism: Toward a Historical Background." Petraglia 3–26.

———. "The Rhetoric of Citation Systems—Part I: The Development of Annotation Structures from the Renaissance to 1900." Ede and Lunsford 337–75.

———. "The Rhetoric of Citation Systems—Part II: Competing Epistemic Values in Citation." Ede and Lunsford 376–98.

———. "The Rhetoric of Mechanical Correctness." Ede and Lunsford 71–98.'

———. "The Rise and Fall of the Modes of Discourse." *On Writing Research: The Braddock Essays, 1975–1998*. Ed. Lisa Ede. Boston: Bedford/St. Martin's, 1999. Print.

Cooper, Marilyn M. "'We Don't Belong Here, Do We?' A Response to 'Lives on the Boundary' and 'The Violence of Literacy.'" *Writing Center Journal* 12.1 (1991): 48–62. Print.

Corbett, Edward P. J., and James L. Golden. *The Rhetoric of Blair, Campbell, and Whately*. Carbondale: Southern Illinois UP, 1990. Print.

Cremin, Lawrence A. *The Transformation of the School: Progressivism in American Education 1876–1957*. New York: Vintage, 1961. Print.

Crowley, Sharon. *Composition in the University: Historical and Polemical Essays*. Pittsburgh: U of Pittsburgh P, 1998.

———. "Composition's Ethic of Service, the Universal Requirement, and the Discourse of Student Need." *Journal of Advanced Composition* 15 (1995): 227–39. Print.

———. "Current-Traditional Rhetoric." *The Encyclopedia of Rhetoric and Composition: Communication from Ancient Times to the Information Age*. Ed. Theresa Enos. New York: Garland, 1996. 156–157. Print.

———. *The Methodical Memory: Invention in Current-Traditional Rhetoric*. Carbondale: Southern Illinois UP, 1990. Print.

———. "The Perilous Life and Times of Freshman English." *Freshman English News* 14.1 (1986): 11–16. Print.

———. "A Personal Essay on Freshman English." *PRE/TEXT* 12 (1991): 156–76. Print.

Cuban, Larry. *How Teachers Taught: Constancy and Change in American Classrooms 1880–1990*. New York: Teachers College Press, 1993. Print.

———. "Reforming Again, Again, and Again." Educational Researcher. 19 (1990): 3–13. Print.

Cushman, Ellen. "The Public Intellectual, Service Learning, and Activist Research." *College English* 61.3 (1999): 328–36. Print.

_____."The Rhetorician as an Agent of Social Change." *College Composition and Communication* 47.1 (1996): 7–28. Print

Cushman, Ellen, et al., eds. *Literacy: A Critical Sourcebook*. New York: Bedford/ St. Martin's. 2001. Print.

Digital Archive of Literacy Narratives (DALN). Web. July 7, 2011.

Darnton, Robert. *The Kiss of Lamourette: Reflections in Cultural History*. New York: Norton, 1990. Print.

Dewey, John. *The Child and the Curriculum*. Chicago: U of Chicago P, 1902. Print.

———. The School and Society. Chicago: U of Chicago P, 1900. Print.

Dobrin, Sidney I. "Paralogic Hermeneutic Theories, Power, and the Possibility for Liberating Pedagogies." *Post-Process Theory: Beyond the Writing-Process Paradigm*. Carbondale: Southern Illinois UP, 1999. 132–48. Print.

———. *Postcomposition*. Carbondale: Southern Illinois UP, 2011. Print.

Downs, Douglas, and Elizabeth Wardle. "Teaching about Writing, Righting Misconceptions: (Re)Envisioning 'First-Year Composition' as 'Introduction to Writing Studies.'" *College Composition and Communication* 58.4 (2007): 552–84. Print.

———. *Writing about Writing: A College Reader*. Boston: Bedford/St. Martin's, 2011. Print.

Dudley, Fred A. "Does Freshman English Take?" *English Journal* 18 (1929): 823–33. Print.

———. "English and Other Teaching." Editorial. *Nation* 19 (1908): 253–54. Print.

———. "The Success of Freshman English." *College English* 2 (1941): 593–98. Print.

Duffy, John. *Writing From These Roots: Literacy in a Hmong-American Community*. Honolulu: U of Hawaii P, 2007. Print.

Ede, Lisa. *Situating Composition: Composition Studies and the Politics of Location*. Carbondale: Southern Illinois UP, 2004. Print.

Ede, Lisa, and Andrea A. Lunsford, eds. *Selected Essays of Robert J. Connors*. New York: Bedford/St. Martin's, 2003. Print.

Elliot, Norbert. *On a Scale: A Social History of Writing Assessment in America*. New York: Lang, 2005. Print.

Ellsworth, Elizabeth Ann. *Teaching Positions: Difference, Pedagogy, and the Power of Address*. New York: Teachers College, 1997. Print.

Eurich, Alvin C. "Should Freshman Composition Be Abolished?" *English Journal* coll. ed. 21 (1932): 211–19. Print.

Finnegan, Ruth. "Literacy versus Non-literacy: The Great Divide?" *Modes of Thought: Essays on Thinking in Western and Non-Western Societies*. Ed. Robin Horton and Ruth Finnegan. London: Faber, 1973. Print.

Fish, Stanley. "What Should Colleges Teach?" Opinion. *New York Times* 24 Aug. 2009. Web. 7 May 2010.

———. *Save the World on Your Own Time*. New York: Oxford UP, 2008. iBooks file.

Fishman, Stephen M., and Lucille Parkinson McCarthy. *John Dewey and the Challenge of Classroom Practice*. New York: Teachers College, 1998. Print.

Fleming, David. *From Form to Meaning: Freshman Composition and the Long Sixties, 1957–1974*. Pittsburgh: U of Pittsburgh P, 2011. Print.

Freire, Paulo. *Pedagogy of the Oppressed*. Trans. Myra Bergman Ramos. New York: Continuum, 1970. Print.

Gallagher, Chris W. *Radical Departures: Composition and Progressive Pedagogy*. Urbana, IL: National Council of Teachers of English, 2002. Print.

Gaillet, Lyneé Lewis, and Thomas P. Miller. "Making Use of the Nineteenth Century: The Writings of Robert Connors and Recent Histories of Rhetoric and Composition." *Rhetoric Review* 20.1/2 (2001): 147–57. Print.

Gee, James Paul. "Progressivism, Critique, and Socially Situated Minds." *The Fate of Progressive Language Policies and Practices*. Ed. Curt Dudley-Marling and Carole Edelsky. Urbana, IL: National Council of Teachers of English, 2001. 31–58.

Gilyard, Keith. ""Composition and the Critical Moment." *Composition Studies in the New Millennium: Rereading the Past, Rewriting the Future*. By Lynn Z. Bloom, Donald A. Daiker, and Edward M. White. Carbondale: Southern Illinois UP, 2003. 65–77. Print.

Giroux, Henry A. "Authority, Intellectuals, and the Politics of Practical Learning." *Teachers College Record* 88.1 (1986): 22–40. Print.

———. *Ideology, Culture, & the Process of Schooling*. Philadelphia: Temple Univ., 1984. Print.

Goggin, Maureen Daly, and Susan Kay Miller. "What is *New* About the 'New Abolitionists': Continuities and Discontinuities in The Great Debate." *Composition Studies* 28.2 (2000): 85–112. Print.

Golden, James L., and Edward P. J. Corbett. *The Rhetoric of Blair, Campbell, and Whately*. Carbondale: Southern Illinois UP, 1990. Print.

Goody, Jack, and Ian Watt. "The Consequences of Literacy." *Language and Social Context*. Ed. Pier Paolo Giglioli. New York: Penguin, 1972. Print.

Grabill, Jeffrey T. *Community Literacy Programs and the Politics of Change*. Albany: State University of New York, 2001. Print.

Graff, Gerald. *Professing Literature: An Institutional History*. Chicago: U of Chicago P, 1987. Print.

Graff, Harvey J. Interview by Doug Dangler. *Writer's Talk*. The Center for the Study and Teaching of Writing at the Ohio State University. Columbus. Mar. 2009. Radio/web. <http://cstw.osu.edu/podcasts/academicwriters/>.

———. *The Labyrinths of Literacy: Reflections on Literacy Past and Present*. 2nd ed. Pittsburgh: U of Pittsburgh P, 1995. Print.

———. *The Legacies of Literacy: Continuities and Contradictions in Western Culture and Society*. Bloomington: Indiana UP, 1987. Print.

———, ed. *Literacy and Historical Development: A Reader*. Carbondale: Southern Illinois UP, 2007. Print.

———. *The Literacy Myth: Cultural Integration and Social Structure in the Nineteenth Century*. New Brunswick, NJ: Transaction, 1991. Print.

———. "The Literacy Myth at Thirty." *The Journal of Social History*. 43 (2010): 635–61. Print.

Graff, Harvey J., and John Duffy. "Literacy Myths." *Encyclopedia of Language and Education*. 2nd ed. Ed. B. V. Street and N. H. Hornberger. London: Springer, 2008. 43–52. Print.

Grafton, Anthony. *The Footnote: A Curious History*. Cambridge, MA: Harvard UP, 1997. Print.

Green, Andrew J. "The Reform of Freshman English." *College English* 2 (1941): 593–98. Print.

Greenbaum, Leonard. "The Tradition of Complaint." *College English* 31 (1969): 174–87. Print.

Guillory, John. *Cultural Capital*. Chicago: U of Chicago P, 1993. Print.

———. "Literary Study and the Modern System of the Disciplines." *Disciplinarity at the fin de siècle*. Ed. Amanda Anderson and Joseph Valente. Princeton, NJ: Princeton UP, 2002. Print.

———. "Who's Afraid of Marcel Proust? The Failure of General Education in the American University." *The Humanities and the Dynamics of Inclusion since World War II*. Ed. David A. Hollinger. Baltimore: Johns Hopkins UP, 2006. Print.

Handbook of English for Engineers. New York: Scott and Foresman, 1913. Print.

Hairston, Maxine. "The Winds of Change: Thomas Kuhn and the Revolution in the Teaching of Writing." *College Composition and Communication* 33 (1982): 76–88. Print.

Halasek, Kay. *A Pedagogy of Possibility: Bakhtinian Perspectives on Composition Studies*. Carbondale: Southern Illinois P, 1999. Print.

Hall, David D. *Culture of Print: Essays in the History of the Book*. Amherst: U of Massachusetts P, 1996. Print.

Hardin, Joe Marshall. *Opening Spaces: Critical Pedagogy and Resistance Theory in Composition*. Albany: State University of New York, 2001. Print.

Harker, Michael. "The Legibility of Literacy in Composition's Great Debate: Revisiting "Romantics on Writing" and the History of Composition." *Literacy in Composition Studies* 1.2 (2013): 20–41. Digital.

Harris, Joseph. "Meet the New Boss, Same as the Old Boss: Class Consciousness in Composition." *College Composition and Communication* 52 (2000): 43–68. Print.

Heath, Shirley Brice. *Ways with Words: Language, Life, and Work in Communities and Classrooms*. Cambridge, UK: Cambridge UP, 1983. Print.

Higham, John. "The Matrix of Specialization." *The Organization of Knowledge in Modern America, 1860–1920*. Ed. Alexandra Oleson and John Voss. Baltimore: Johns Hopkins UP, 1979. Print.

hooks, bell. *Teaching to Transgress: Education as the Practice of Freedom*. New York: Routledge, 1994. Print.

Holinger, David A, ed. *The Humanities and the Dynamics of Inclusion since World War II*. Baltimore: Johns Hopkins UP, 2006. Print.

Holmes, Steven. "Actants, Agents, and Assemblages: Delivery and Writing in an Age of New Media." (2013) All Dissertations. Paper 1086.

Hoover, R. M. "Taps for Freshman English?" *College Composition and Communication* 25 (1974): 149–54. Print.

Horner, Bruce. *Terms of Work for Composition: A Materialist Critique*. Albany: SUNY P, 2000. Print.

Hurlbut, B. S. "College requirements in English." *Twenty years of school and college English*. Ed. A. S. Hill. Cambridge, MA: Harvard UP, 1896. Print.

Johnson, Nan. *Nineteenth-Century Rhetoric in North America*. Carbondale: Southern Illinois UP, 1991. Print.

Journal of Higher Education. "The Reporter." Washington DC: American Association for Higher Education, 1937. Print.

Kane, Thomas S. "Rhetoric and the 'Problem' of Composition." *College English* 22.7 (1961): 503–6. Print.

Kates, Susan. *Activist Rhetorics and American Higher Education, 1885–1937*. Carbondale: Southern Illinois UP, 2001. Print.

Katz, Michael B. *Class, Bureaucracy, and Schools: The Illusion of Educational Change in America*. New York: Praeger, 1975. Print.

———. *The Irony of Early School Reform: Educational Innovation in Mid-Nineteenth Century Massachusetts*. Cambridge: Harvard UP, 1968. Print.

———. *Reconstructing American Education*. Cambridge, MA: Harvard UP, 1987. Print.

Knoblauch, C. H., and Lil Brannon. *Critical Teaching and the Idea of Literacy*. Portsmouth, NH: Boynton/Cook, 1993. Print.

Lange, Paulus. "What Price English?" *The Journal of Higher Education* 9.8 (1938): 424–28. Print.

Levine, Kenneth. *The Social Context of Literacy*. London: Routledge, 1986. Print.

Literacy Studies@OSU (LS@OSU). "Graduate Interdisciplinary Specialization." Web. November 22, 2011. <http://literacystudies.osu.edu/academics/gis.cfm>.

Lounsbury, Thomas R. "Compulsory Composition in Colleges." *Harper's Monthly Magazine*. Nov. 1911: 866–80. Print.

Lunsford, Andrea A., Helene Moglen, and James Slevin. *The Right to Literacy*. New York: MLA, 1990.

Manchester, Frederick A. "Freshman English Once More." *The English Journal* 6.5 (1917): 295–307. Print.

———. "Freshman English Once More—Concluded." *The English Journal* 6.6 (1917): 384–398. Print.

———. "Moral Education and History." *The Freeman*. 18.7 (1968). Web. 11 Dec. 2011. <http://www.thefreemanonline.org/featured/moral-education-and-history/>.

Marsden, George M., and Bradley J. Longfield, eds. *The Secularization of the Academy*. New York: Oxford UP, 1992. Print.

Masters, Thomas M. *Practicing Writing: The Postwar Discourse of Freshman English*. Pittsburgh: U of Pittsburgh P, 2004. Print.

McKenzie, D. F. *Bibliography and The Sociology of Texts*. Cambridge, UK: Cambridge UP, 1999. Print.

The Michigan Committee on the Articulation of High-School and College English. *Preparation for College English: An Interpretation of College Entrance Standards in English*. Ed. Clarence D. Thorpe. Ann Arbor: U of Michigan P, 1942. Print.

Min-Zhan, Lu, and Bruce Horner. "The Problematic of Experience: Redefining Critical Work in Ethnography and Pedagogy." *College English* 60.3 (1998): 257–77. Print.

Moghtader, Michael, Alanna Cotch, and Kristen Hague. "The First-Year Composition Requirement Revisited: A Survey." *College Composition and Communication*. 52.3 (2001): 455–67. Print.

Murray, Donald M. "Finding Your Own Voice: Teaching Composition in an Age of Dissent." *College Composition and Communication* 20.2 (1969): 118–23. Print.

Naumberg, Margaret. *The Child and the World: Dialogs in Modern Education*. New York: Harcourt, 1928. Print.

North, Stephen. *The Making of Knowledge in Composition: Portrait of an emerging field*. Upper Montclair, NJ: Boynton/Cook, 1987. Print.

Noyes, Edward Simpson. "The New Type of Tests in Composition." *English Leaflet* 44.392 (1945): 49–58. Print.

Noyes, Edward Simpson, and John Marshall Stalnaker. *Report on the English Examination of June 1937: A Description of the Procedures Used in Preparing and Reading the Examination in English and an Analysis of the Results of the Reading*. New York: College Entrance Examination Board, 1938. Print.

Oleson, Alexander, and John Voss, eds. *The Organization of Knowledge in Modern America, 1860–1920*. Baltimore: Johns Hopkins UP, 1979. Print.

Olson, Gary A. "History, 'Praxis,' and Change: Paulo Freire and the Politics of Literacy." *Journal of Advanced Composition* 12.1 (1992): 1–14. Print.

Oppenheim, Nathan. *The Development of the Child*. New York: Macmillan, 1910. Print.

Petraglia, Joseph, ed. *Reconceiving Writing, Rethinking Writing Instruction*. Mahwah, NJ: Lawrence Erlbaum Associates, 1996. Print.

Reuben, Julie A. *The Making of the Modern University: Intellectual Transformation and the Marginalization of Morality*. Chicago: U of Chicago P, 1996. Print.

Rhodes, Jacqueline. "Composition in the University: Historical and Polemical Essays." *Rhetoric Society Quarterly* 30.1. (2000): 96–98. Print.

Rice, Joseph Mayer. *The Public-School System of the United States*. New York: Arno, 1969. Print.

Rice, Warner G. "Articulation of the Secondary School and the College." *College English* 2.2 (1940) 136–45. Print.

———. "A Proposal for the Abolition of Freshman English, As It Is Now Commonly Taught, from the College Curriculum." *College English* 21 (1960): 361–67. Print.

Roemer, Marjorie, Lucille M. Schultz, and Russel K. Durst. "Reframing the Great Debate on First-Year Writing." *College Composition and Communication* 50 (1998): 54–70. Print.

Rose, Mike. "The Language of Exclusion: Writing Instruction at the University." *The Norton Book of Composition Studies*. Ed. Susan Miller. New York: Norton, 2009. Print.

———. *The Mind at Work: Valuing the Intelligence of the American Worker*. New York: Viking, 2004. Print.

———. "Narrowing the Mind and Page: Remedial Writers and Cognitive Reductionism." *College Composition and Communication* 39.3 (1988): 267–302. Print.

———. *Possible Lives: The Promise of Public Education in America*. Boston: Houghton Mifflin, 1995. Print.

———. *An Open Language: Selected Writing on Literacy, Learning, and Opportunity*. Boston: Bedford/St. Martin's, 2006. Print.

Rose, Shirley K. "The Role of Scholarly Citations in Disciplinary Economies." *Perspectives On Plagiarism and Intellectual Property in a Postmodern World*. Eds. Lise Buranen and Alice M. Roy. New York: SUNY P, 1999. Print.

Rudolph, Frederick. *The American College & University: A History*. Athens: U of Georgia P, 1962. Print.

Rugg, Harold, and Ann Schumaker. *The Child-Centered School*. Yonkers, NY: World Book, 1928. Print.

Russell, David R. "Activity Theory and Its Implications for Writing Instruction." Petraglia 51–77.

———. "Romantics on Writing: Liberal Culture and the Abolition of Composition Courses." *Rhetoric Review* 6 (1988): 132–148. Print.

———. *Writing in the Academic Disciplines: A Curricular History*. Carbondale: Southern Illinois UP, 2002. Print.

Sánchez, Raúl. *The Function of Theory in Composition Studies*. New York: SUNY P, 2005. Print.

———. Rev. of *Composition in the University*, by Sharon Crowley. *Journal of Advanced Composition*. 19.4 (1999).

Scribner, Sylvia, and Michael Cole. *The Psychology of Literacy*. Cambridge, MA: Harvard UP, 1981. Print.

———. "Unpackaging Literacy." *Social Science Information* 17.1 (1978): 19–40. Print.

Seitz, David. "Hard Lessons Learned Since the First Generation of Critical Pedagogy." *College English* 64.4 (2002): 503–12. Print.

Shaughnessy, Mina. *Errors & Expectations: a guide for the teacher of basic writing.* New York: Oxford UP, 1977. Print.

Shor, Ira. *Critical Teaching and Everyday Life.* Boston: South End, 1980. Print.

———. "Our Apartheid: Writing Instruction & Inequality." *Journal of Basic Writing* 16.1 (1997): 91–104. Digital.

Shumway, David R., and Craig Dionne, eds. *Disciplining English: Alternative Histories, Critical Perspectives.* New York: SUNY P, 2002. Print.

Sirc, Geoffrey Michael. *English Composition as a Happening.* Logan, UT: Utah State UP, 2002. Print.

Smit, David W. *The End of Composition Studies.* Carbondale: Southern Illinois UP, 2004. Print.

Smith, Ron. "The Composition Requirement Today: A Report on a Nationwide Survey of Four-Year Colleges and Universities." *College Composition and Communication* 25.2 (1974): 138–48. Print.

Steinhoff, William. "Some Remarks on the Future of the Required Course in Freshman Composition." *College Composition and Communication* 12 (1961): 23–26. Print.

Stephens, Kate. "A Critical Discussion of the 'New Literacy Studies.'" *The British Journal of Educational Studies.* 48.1 (2000): 10–23. Print.

Street, Brian V. *Literacy in theory and practice.* Cambridge, UK: Cambridge UP, 1984. Print.

———. "What's 'new' in New Literacy Studies? Critical approaches to literacy in theory and practice." *Current Issues in Comparative Education* 5.2 (2003): 77–91. Print.

Taylor, Warner. "Should the Course in Freshman Composition Be Abolished?" *English Journal* coll. ed. 21 (1932): 301–11. Print.

Thomas, Joseph M., Frederick A. Manchester, and Franklin W. Scott. *Composition for College Students: A guide for the study and effective writing of good English, with abundant illustrative examples from many authors.* 5th edition. New York: Macmillan, 1948. Print.

Thurber, E. A. "College Composition." *The Nation* 6 Sep. 1915: 328–29. Print.

———. "Composition in Our Colleges." *The English Journal* 4.1 (1915): 9–14. Print.

Time Warner Cable. "Marketing Summary: Rick Nash Adult Literacy Campaign." Web. 24 Nov. 2011. <http://www.ctam.com/html/markawards/pastwinners/2009/44-15810.aspx>.

Turner, James. "Secularization and Sacralization: Speculations on Some Religious Origins of the Secular Humanities Curriculum, 1850–1880." *The Secularization of the Academy.* Ed. George M. Marsden and Bradley J. Longfield. New York: Oxford UP, 1992. Print.

Tyack, David. *The One Best System.* Cambridge, MA: Harvard UP, 1974. Print.

———. "Public School Reform: Policy Talk and Institutional Practice." *American Journal of Education* 100.1 (1991): 1–19.

Tyack, David, and Larry Cuban. *Tinkering toward Utopia: A Century of Public School Reform.* Cambridge, MA: Harvard UP, 1995. Print.

Ulman, Lewis H. *Things, Thoughts, Words, and Actions: The Problem of Language in Late Eighteenth-Century British Rhetorical Theory.* Carbondale: Southern Illinois UP, 1994. Print.

Veysey, Laurence R. *The Emergence of the American University*. Chicago: U of Chicago P, 1965. Print.

Villanueva, Victor. *Bootstraps: From an American Academic of Color*. Urbana, IL: National Council of Teachers of English, 1993. Print.

Vincent, David. *The Rise of Mass Literacy: Reading and Writing in Modern Europe*. Malden, MA: Blackwell, 2000. Print.

Volosinov, Valentin N. *Marxism and the Philosophy of Language*. Trans. Ladislav Matejka and I.R. Titunik. Cambridge, MA: Harvard UP, 1973. Print.

Williams, James D., ed. *Visions and Revisions: Continuity and Change in Rhetoric and Composition*. Carbondale: Southern Illinois UP, 2002. Print.

INDEX